DISCIPL

"The gospel. Obedient disc. offering a stirring vision of what the always-reforming church has been and can become, *Discipleship in Community* seizes the pulsating heart of Scripture. It avoids scholarly minutiae, offering practical advice for how individuals and congregations can remain faithfully rooted in the activity of the Father, Son, and Holy Spirit."

—**Matthew W. Bates,** Quincy University

"When I return from speaking at a Churches of Christ event and tell my pastor or academic friends, they often ask me, "What do the Churches of Christ believe?" From now on I will say, read this book. But this book will do something else: it will introduce the Churches of Christ to the broader movement with which they have many deep affinities—evangelicalism. That will be good for all of us."

—**Scot McKnight,** Northern Seminary

"In an age in which religious affiliation continues to wither, Christian communities are burdened with the charge of effectively communicating who they are and why that matters. This book does precisely that for the heirs of the Stone-Campbell Movement by lifting up discipleship not simply as a theme from the past, but as the way forward to a hopeful future. I commend the authors for approaching their tradition with such care and concern. This book represents institutional charity—that is, love of a tradition—at its best."

—**Daniel Castelo,** Seattle Pacific University

"*Discipleship in Community* is a vital and careful plea for the reexamination of theological commitments within Churches of Christ. A fair and attentive book, the authors offer constructive proposals for a new, yet thoroughly biblical, vision of how to emerge from the current crisis facing those who embrace the restoration tradition."

—**Arthur Sutherland,** Loyola University Maryland

"In *Discipleship in Community*, Powell, Hicks, and McKinzie provide a perceptive analysis of the key theological ideas of our heritage. Beyond analysis, the gift of this book is its usefulness in showing how these historic ideas may shape our hearts and lives for and through obedience. In this sweet participation in the practical life of the church, we follow Jesus, who makes all things new."

—**Carisse Mickey Berryhill,** Abilene Christian University

"The future of any tradition depends on its ability to draw upon the resources of its own past to overcome or adapt to whatever challenges the present and future may bring. That is precisely what this volume does. Churches of Christ need not surrender their unique identity in order to transcend the liabilities that beset many of their congregations. Rather, they may affirm the keenest insights of their founders while moving beyond them in ways that draw upon the equally keen insights of the broader Christian tradition, both past and present."

—**John Nugent,** Great Lakes Christian College

"We are truly indebted to Powell, Hicks, and McKinzie for a timely and thought-provoking book. I boldly predict that this book will spark renewed theological reflection in the fellowship of Churches of Christ and beyond."

—**Edward J. Robinson,** author of *Show Us How You Do It: Marshall Keeble and the Rise of Black Churches of Christ in the United States, 1914-1968*

"Disciple making is the core mission of the local church. I commend this book to everyone within Churches of Christ who hungers to learn more about disciple making and the best path for churches into the future."

—**Bobby Harrington,** point-leader of discipleship.org and renew.org

"In *Discipleship in Community*, Powell, Hicks, and McKinzie offer a convincing theological vision for Churches of Christ. Deeply grounded in their knowledge of the history of the Churches of Christ and the larger Stone-Campbell Restoration movement, their book brings Churches of Christ into dialogue with the early Christian communities in and beyond the New Testament period, and with other Christian communities today. Highly recommended, not just for Churches of Christ folks, but for other Christians intent on understanding the ethos and directions of their churches."

—**Ted Campbell,** Southern Methodist University

DISCIPLESHIP
IN COMMUNITY

DISCIPLESHIP IN COMMUNITY

A THEOLOGICAL VISION for the FUTURE

MARK E. POWELL

JOHN MARK HICKS

GREG MCKINZIE

Abilene Christian University Press

DISCIPLESHIP IN COMMUNITY
A Theological Vision for the Future

Copyright © 2020 by Mark E. Powell, John Mark Hicks, and Greg McKinzie

ISBN 978-1-68426-410-1 | LCCN 2019056910

Printed in the United States of America

ALL RIGHTS RESERVED
No part of this publication may be reproduced, stored in a retrieval system, or transmitted in any form by any means—electronic, mechanical, photocopying, recording, or otherwise—without prior written consent.

All scripture quotations, unless otherwise indicated, are taken from the Holy Bible, New International Version®, NIV®. Copyright © 1973, 1978, 1984, 2011 by Biblica, Inc.™ Used by permission of Zondervan. All rights reserved worldwide.

LIBRARY OF CONGRESS CATALOGING-IN-PUBLICATION DATA
Names: Powell, Mark E., author. | Hicks, John Mark, author. | McKinzie, Greg, 1982- author.
Title: Discipleship in community : a theological vision for the future / Mark E. Powell, John Mark Hicks and Greg McKinzie.
Description: Abilene, Texas : Abilene Christian University Press, 2020. | Includes bibliographical references.
Identifiers: LCCN 2019056910 | ISBN 9781684264100 (paperback)
Subjects: LCSH: Churches of Christ. | Christian life. | Theology, Doctrinal. | Christianity—21st century.
Classification: LCC BX7076 .P69 2020 | DDC 230/.6634—dc23
LC record available at https://lccn.loc.gov/2019056910

Cover design by ThinkPen Design
Interior text design by Sandy Armstrong, Strong Design

For information contact:
Abilene Christian University Press
ACU Box 29138
Abilene, Texas 79699

1-877-816-4455
www.acupressbooks.com

20 21 22 23 24 25 26 / 7 6 5 4 3 2 1

CONTENTS

Acknowledgments 9

Chapter One
    An Invitation to Discipleship 11

Chapter Two
    Starting with God: The Trinity 25

Chapter Three
    Participating in God's Story: Eschatology 47

Chapter Four
    Encountering the Living Word: Scripture 69

Chapter Five
    Pursuing Intentional Discipleship: The Believers Church 91

Chapter Six
    Experiencing God in Community: The Sacraments 115

Chapter Seven
    Participating in God's Purposes: Mission 137

Chapter Eight
    Theological Commitments in Churches of Christ 159

Response
    by Lauren Smelser White 165

Response
    by Stanley Talbert 172

Response
    by Carson E. Reed 177

Appendix One:
    Rules of Faith and Ecumenical Creeds of the Early Church 185

Appendix Two:
    Alexander Campbell's "Summary View of the Christian System of Facts" .. 189

ACKNOWLEDGMENTS

This book seeks both to describe who Churches of Christ have been and to propose a constructive vision for the future. Given the difficulty of the task, it was clear from the beginning that this should be a multiauthor work. Each author wrote two main chapters (Chapters Two to Seven), and each chapter was revised based on the input of the other two authors. In addition, Mark Powell wrote Chapters One and Eight and served as the general editor of the work. As is evident from the chapters, the authors have different approaches, styles, and temperaments, and yet the goal was to provide a coherent vision on which we all could agree. We believe that the result of this process has been a better and more comprehensive proposal. As an editorial decision, the authors used gender-neutral language, but we did not alter historical quotations.

The authors sincerely thank the three respondents, who engaged this book in a thoughtful and timely fashion. The responses offer important additional perspectives and, we believe, show the fruitfulness of the primary proposal. We also thank two graduate assistants, Robert Ogden and Eli Randolph, who provided valuable support in the research and production of this book. Of course, we are grateful to Jason Fikes and everyone at ACU Press for their quality work and for agreeing to make this proposal available to a larger audience.

Chapter One

AN INVITATION TO DISCIPLESHIP

To God our Father, through the great Author of the Christian faith, who has preserved us in health to this day of affliction and great distress, be everlasting thanks for the renewing of our minds by the Holy Spirit, and for the hope of the regeneration of our bodies, of the heavens and of the earth, at the appearance of the Almighty Regenerator, who comes to make all things new!—Amen.

—Alexander Campbell, *The Christian System* (1839)

This book is an invitation to two separate but related journeys. First, it is an invitation to a conversation about the theological framework and commitments of the Stone-Campbell movement and, in particular, Churches of Christ. This invitation is especially relevant for those who care about and are indebted to the movement. Second, and more importantly, this book is an invitation to everyone to participate in what we take to be the heart of the Stone-Campbell movement, Churches of Christ, and the Christian faith as a whole: a life of simple, authentic discipleship.

Churches of Christ are conservative heirs of the Stone-Campbell movement, an American restoration movement that emerged in the early nineteenth century and produced, in addition to Churches of Christ, the Christian Church (Disciples of Christ) and the Christian Churches/Churches of Christ. The early leaders of the Stone-Campbell movement, including Thomas Campbell, Alexander Campbell, Barton W. Stone, and Walter Scott, sought to restore the simple teachings and practices of the New Testament church, or what Alexander Campbell called the "ancient order of things." Their pursuit of restoration, though, was always about more than recovering ancient forms of church life and worship. They believed that by restoring the forms of the early church, they would also restore the spirit and dynamism of the early church. Further, they believed the restoration of the early church would promote greater ends, like faithfulness to God, Christian unity, participation in God's mission, and freedom of conscience.

The central concerns of the Stone-Campbell movement continue to be compelling today, but like most other Western Christian traditions, the Stone-Campbell movement and Churches of Christ are experiencing a time of identity crisis and transition. The March 2018 edition of *The Christian Chronicle*, which illustrates this crisis, was dedicated to addressing the question "What is a Church of Christ?" Similarly, the authors of this book and C. Leonard Allen participated in a session at the 2013 Thomas Olbricht Christian Scholars' Conference titled "What Are / Should Be the Theological Emphases of Churches of Christ?" Our question could be stated in other ways as well. What does it mean to engage in theology from a Stone-Campbell restoration perspective? Where have we been and where are we going as a religious movement? These questions are more specific, but they are similar to the one raised in *The Christian Chronicle*.

In times of crisis and disorientation, there is typically a strong desire to cease theological reflection and so-called navel gazing and get back to the pressing, practical work at hand. This desire is

An Invitation to Discipleship

understandable and can even be a good way to proceed for a time, but the hard intellectual work remains. Interestingly, in Churches of Christ, the desire to "get back to work" and the necessary intellectual task may actually coalesce. It is our contention that the orienting theological concern of the Stone-Campbell movement and Churches of Christ can be summarized by the word *discipleship*.[1] Early on, those associated with the movement, especially those influenced by Alexander Campbell, preferred to be called Disciples of Christ or simply Disciples, and one branch of the movement continues to go by the name Disciples of Christ.[2] Even among the conservative heirs of the movement like Churches of Christ, renewal efforts and publications often stress the term *discipleship*.[3] Clearly, a concern for discipleship is deeply embedded in our DNA, but it is also a central biblical theme and one that helps set the church on mission. We propose that the best way to address our current disorientation is (1) to return to an emphasis on discipleship in our theological reflection and (2) to actually get back to the work of discipleship. It should also be stressed that

---

[1] Examples of other orienting theological concerns include justification by faith (Lutheran theology), sovereignty of God (Reformed theology), holiness (Methodist theology), and liberation (liberation theology). Additionally, individual theologians often stress an orienting theological concern that brings cohesion and relevance to their presentation of the Christian faith.

[2] The ongoing prominence of discipleship as an orienting concern for the Christian Church (Disciples of Christ) is illustrated by Mark G. Toulouse's book *Joined in Discipleship: The Shaping of Contemporary Disciples Identity*, rev. ed. (St. Louis: Chalice Press, 1997).

[3] For instance, beginning in the 1970s, a movement that would eventually become the International Churches of Christ (ICOC) sought to reform mainline Churches of Christ through a "discipling ministry." Leaders of mainline churches strongly criticized the tactics of the ICOC, and ICOC leaders have publicly repented of sinful attitudes and unhealthy methods, but the fact that discipleship was a central theme for reform here is instructive. Currently, another renewal movement among conservative Stone-Campbell traditions, called Renew, emphasizes the importance of discipleship (see http://www.renew.org). Consider also the title of Lee Camp's popular book *Mere Discipleship*, rev. ed. (Grand Rapids, MI: Brazos, 2008).

discipleship includes reliance on God and participating in God's work in God's timing. Prayerfully waiting on God is an important spiritual exercise during times of disorientation. Theological reflection in Churches of Christ gains traction not when it is an exercise in abstract speculation, but when it arises from and aids authentic discipleship.

Allan J. McNicol, longtime New Testament professor at Austin Graduate School of Theology in Texas, made a similar observation in his address at the *Restoration Quarterly* breakfast during the 1998 AAR/SBL Annual Meeting.[4] McNicol affirmed that the crisis facing the Stone-Campbell movement is a real one, as one popular interpretation of the restoration plea is inherently flawed: "We now know, after two centuries of critical biblical scholarship, that the idea that there is hidden behind all the accidental data of the New Testament a Platonic model for every detail of the ideal church is mistaken." However, McNicol continues, this does not mean that there are no other (or better) ways of conceiving the restoration plea: "[F]ollowing the direction of a number of our earlier leaders, we would be well advised to understand Restorationism, not as an end in itself, but as a means toward a goal, namely, shaping us into conformity with the gospel of Christ through a life of obedience toward God carried out within the church." McNicol goes on to propose that the "fundamental theological sensibility" of the Stone-Campbell movement is the "essential insight that one cannot be a Christian without living the obedient life of discipleship in a visible community of faith."[5]

As the title *Discipleship in Community* suggests, we fundamentally agree with McNicol's proposal. In addition to his strong

---

[4] This address was later published: Allan J. McNicol, "Is the Stone-Campbell Movement an Identifiable Theological Tradition?" *Restoration Quarterly* 41, no. 2 (1999): 65–70.

[5] McNicol, "Is the Stone-Campbell Movement an Identifiable Theological Tradition?" 69.

correlation between discipleship and the church community, we also emphasize two other referents for the term *community*. First and foremost, discipleship begins and ends with the divine community—the Triune God who is Father, Son, and Holy Spirit. In fact, we define discipleship as participation in the life and mission of the Trinitarian God. Such participation includes a life of worship, spiritual formation, and sharing in God's mission. Second, we affirm with McNicol that God intends for discipleship to occur within the church community. Unlike some evangelical traditions, Churches of Christ have always emphasized regular participation in the life of the local church as essential for discipleship. Third, community also refers to those communities throughout the world where Christians live, work, and play. Discipleship is an invitation to follow God into the world and to participate in God's mission of offering life and salvation to all. Discipleship occurs as Christians go into the world and proclaim the gospel in words and actions.

Discipleship in community is an orienting concern for the Stone-Campbell movement and Churches of Christ, but this theological emphasis must be further unpacked. To do so, we explore six theological convictions of early Stone-Campbell leaders that, we propose, continue to be constructive commitments for Churches of Christ today:

1. A Trinitarian vision of God
2. An eschatological outlook
3. A strong biblical orientation in our teaching and spirituality
4. The Believers Church tradition
5. The sacramental presence and working of God, especially in baptism and the Lord's Supper
6. The church's participation in God's mission

These six commitments are important because of the way they turn our focus to God and promote healthy, authentic Christian discipleship. Clearly, this list needs explanation and further elaboration, and even lifelong members of Churches of Christ may be unfamiliar with some of our vocabulary. We do hope, however, that an explanation of this list of theological commitments will sound both familiar and compelling.

FALSE STARTS

Before further summarizing these six commitments, it is helpful to consider other ways of addressing the fundamental theological emphases of Churches of Christ that we intentionally set aside. First, one could argue that Stone-Campbell theology is characterized by a particular theological method or form of biblical interpretation. When one follows this method or hermeneutic, it is argued, then one is engaged in Stone-Campbell theological reflection; but if one abandons this method or hermeneutic, one has left the Stone-Campbell theological fold. A number of practices and commitments of early Stone-Campbell leaders could be presented as representative of this approach. For instance, the early leaders sought unity around the basic beliefs, practices, and even vocabulary of the New Testament that, it was argued, any reasonable person would affirm. The early leaders followed the regulative principle of biblical interpretation, which affirms biblical commands, examples, and necessary inferences but views silence as prohibitive, especially in regard to worship assemblies. Following Alexander Campbell's influential "Sermon on the Law," the early leaders viewed the New Testament, and especially the books of Acts through Revelation, as a constitution or blueprint for the church today that should be read as a legal document or a scientific book of facts.

However, it is a mistake to reduce Stone-Campbell theology to a particular method or hermeneutic, and this error can be traced in two different directions. First, one can affirm the methods and philosophical assumptions of the early Stone-Campbell leaders and still reject their theological conclusions. For instance, in the early nineteenth century, leaders associated with the Christian Connection held similar views as the Stone-Campbell leaders about theological method and biblical interpretation, but they also emphasized anti-Trinitarianism, quarterly celebration of the Lord's Supper, and the importance of a conversion experience.[6] These differences involve two key theological commitments of Churches of Christ on the Trinity and the sacraments (that is, the function and importance of baptism and the Lord's Supper). Further, the regulative principle of biblical interpretation is followed by most heirs of the Reformed tradition that emerged during the Protestant Reformation, including Presbyterians and Baptists, but theological differences remain between these groups and Churches of Christ. Agreement on theological method and biblical interpretation does not guarantee agreement on theological conclusions.

And the second reason it is inaccurate to reduce Stone-Campbell theology to a particular theological method or hermeneutic is that today, many heirs of the Stone-Campbell movement qualify or reject the philosophical assumptions of early Stone-Campbell leaders, but still affirm their primary theological conclusions. For example, to simply repeat biblical language that Jesus is the "Messiah" and "Son of God" without addressing what is intended by this language overlooks important issues in Christology, which Christians historically (the authors of this book included) have viewed as foundational for Christian faith. The best of our theological arguments appeal not simply to biblical

---

[6] See Thomas H. Olbricht, "Christian Connection," in *The Encyclopedia of the Stone-Campbell Movement*, ed. Douglas A. Foster, Paul M. Blowers, Anthony L. Dunnavant, and D. Newell Williams (Grand Rapids: Eerdmans, 2004): 190–91.

silence but also to historical, theological, and practical reasons for our beliefs and practices. Instead of flattening Scripture to fit the mold of a constitution or blueprint, contemporary biblical scholars argue for a more careful reading of Scripture that accounts for issues like narrative context and genre. In other words, much of Scripture is not law and should not be read as such. Stone-Campbell heirs who question the philosophical assumptions of their forebears, however, still affirm many of the theological commitments of the early Stone-Campbell leaders. Disagreement on matters of theological method and hermeneutics does not exclude agreement on theological conclusions.

Careful reflection on theological method, epistemology, and hermeneutics is important, and the authors of this work are deeply engaged in these discussions. Nonetheless, issues of theological method and biblical interpretation are always secondary to actual theological conclusions. Therefore, rather than focus on theological method, epistemology, and hermeneutics, we choose to emphasize central theological commitments of early Stone-Campbell leaders and Churches of Christ today.

A second approach that we forego is to simply highlight and defend traditional distinctive practices of Churches of Christ, especially in regard to church life and worship. Such distinctive practices include believers' baptism for the forgiveness of sins and the reception of the Spirit, weekly celebration of the Lord's Supper, a cappella singing in corporate worship, and autonomous congregations led by a plurality of elders. Recently, some congregations have loosened their commitment to some of these practices, but by and large, these practices continue to characterize Churches of Christ today. Focusing on distinctive practices to the exclusion of the theological commitments that give reason and meaning to them, however, can lead to a stale, human-centered view of these practices and can divorce these practices from a life of discipleship.

We discuss traditional practices of Churches of Christ, but we do so within a larger theological framework that undergirds these practices.

THEOLOGICAL COMMITMENTS: A SUMMARY

The following chapters present the theological commitments of Churches of Christ in more detail, but some brief comments should help by way of introduction. If discipleship is participation in the life and mission of the Trinitarian God, then attention must be given to the Christian vision of God as Father, Son, and Holy Spirit (the Trinity) and what God has done and is doing in the redemption of all creation (eschatology). By starting with the Trinity and eschatology, we are starting with God and submitting ourselves to God's work in the world.

Admittedly, Churches of Christ have not always emphasized the doctrine of the Trinity. The Stone-Campbell movement emerged during a time when Trinitarian doctrine was viewed as both overly abstract and divisive. Some of the movement's early leaders, such as Alexander Campbell, sought to avoid speculative and non-biblical theological language—including the word *Trinity* itself—though his own position essentially followed the classic Trinitarian one. Others, such as Barton W. Stone, explicitly rejected the doctrine of the Trinity, but Stone's position soon became marginal—at least in the conservative side of the movement. Many of the movement's leaders could be described as implicit and irenic Trinitarians. They implicitly maintained a Trinitarian view more so than explicitly presented one, and they viewed the doctrine of the Trinity as a matter of theological opinion. As will be demonstrated in Chapter Two, however, a number of the movement's key leaders emphasized a Trinitarian view of God in their writings.

There has been a renaissance of Trinitarian theology since the middle of the twentieth century. Rather than being viewed as overly abstract, today, the Trinity is viewed (much like it was in the early church) as central to Christian belief and practice. Rather than being viewed as divisive, today, it is viewed as a unifying doctrine (again, like it was in the early church). We see these developments as important ones for the future of Churches of Christ and spell out the implications of starting with the Trinity in Chapter Two and throughout the book.

Eschatology refers to the doctrine of last things and Christian hope. Similar to the doctrine of the Trinity, the study of eschatology has experienced widespread resurgence during the last half of the twentieth century. The earliest Christians clearly recognized that in Jesus Christ, God's reign is breaking into the world and is both a present reality and a future hope. Since our future hope includes union with God and the redemption of creation, eschatology is not just about last things but encapsulates the entire biblical story from creation to new creation. Further, Christian hope gives direction to and motivation for a life of discipleship in the present. Alexander Campbell, David Lipscomb, and James A. Harding held various millennial views, but they all emphasized, anticipated, and were motivated by a future hope that includes the cosmic renewal of creation. The centrality of eschatology, Christian hope, and participating in God's story is presented in Chapter Three and emphasized throughout the book.

In many ways, the first two chapters follow the rules of faith and ecumenical creeds of the early church in the second through fifth centuries. The rules of faith were summaries of Christian belief that varied in wording and were less fixed than formal creeds. Typically, both rules of faith and early creeds were structured around the Christian vision of God as Father, Son, and Holy Spirit, and they traced God's work from creation to new creation (see Appendix One). Interestingly, Alexander Campbell followed a similar approach by presenting a "Summary View of the Christian

System of Facts" in *The Christian System* (see Appendix Two). By starting with the Trinity and eschatology, we intentionally follow the early church and ground Stone-Campbell theological commitments in the historic vision of God and God's work in creation and redemption.

The next four commitments are clearly recognizable to anyone who is familiar with Churches of Christ. Churches of Christ are biblical, a Believers Church tradition, sacramental, and missional. Scripture has always been the most important theological source for Churches of Christ, and Churches of Christ have produced an impressive number of biblical scholars. Further, the spiritual formation of members in Churches of Christ is deeply shaped by studying and meditating on Scripture. In Chapter Four, we engage and deepen this commitment to Scripture by proposing that, in keeping with the other theological commitments, Scripture is best read in light of the Trinity (the Christian vision of God) and eschatology (the story of God's redemption of creation). Further, Scripture is best read within a community of disciples who are intentionally pursuing spiritual formation and participating in God's mission. When reading Scripture, it matters who we are (as those seeking God and the Christian virtues) and where we are (as those participating in God's mission, especially in humble locations and among vulnerable people). Good biblical interpretation is a communal exercise, where the church seeks the Spirit's guidance and together discerns the Word of God.

Churches of Christ are a Believers Church tradition, which is an alternative to Catholic and mainline Protestant visions of the church. In the Believers Church tradition, becoming a Christian is far more than experiencing baptism as an infant and being a good citizen of a Christian nation. Becoming a Christian is a decision that adult believers make through their confession of faith and baptism. Further, Christians embrace a life of intentional discipleship that includes regular participation in the worship assembly, ongoing spiritual formation, and participation in God's mission. In Chapter Five, we explore the Believers Church tradition in general, and Churches of Christ in particular, by considering how Churches of Christ understand the four classic marks of the church as presented in the Nicene Creed and grounded in the New Testament witness: the church is one, holy, universal (or catholic), and apostolic.

Those in the Believers Church tradition usually practice believer's baptism, and Churches of Christ are no exception in this regard. But unlike many Believers Church traditions, Churches of Christ hold that baptism is more than just a visible (and optional) sign of saving faith. Rather, believer's baptism is a means of grace, where one is united with Christ and receives forgiveness of sins and the indwelling of the Holy Spirit. Further, weekly participation in the Lord's Supper has been a prominent feature of worship in the Stone-Campbell movement from its beginnings. In the Lord's Supper, we share table fellowship with God through our risen and present Lord, we feed on and remain in Christ by the working of the Spirit, and we celebrate what God has done for our salvation. In Chapter Six, we present the sacramental commitment of Churches of Christ and offer practical suggestions for deepening this commitment.

From the beginning, the Stone-Campbell movement has held a deep concern for participation in God's mission. In fact, the Stone-Campbell plea for unity through restoration was always for the sake of mission. In Chapter Seven, we explore and develop the missional emphasis of Churches of Christ by challenging all Christians, not just those engaged in cross-cultural mission efforts, to participate in God's mission in the world. Such participation includes humbling ourselves and walking alongside those on the margins of society. Further, we argue that the desire to restore a more biblical church should lead to the restoration of a more missional church, including one that is able to adapt to diverse cultural contexts today.

No one of these six theological commitments are unique to Churches of Christ, but the combination of them does appear to be unique to the conservative heirs of the Stone-Campbell movement. Regardless, our goal is not to be unique, per se, but to be faithful to God and present a healthy theological vision for Churches of Christ. The final chapter presents a concise summary of the six theological commitments and is available as a web document at https://hst.edu/tc. We hope this summary will be useful to churches as they educate both church members and interested observers about Churches of Christ.

As stated earlier, we hope this book promotes a conversation and encourages renewed theological reflection in Churches of Christ. But we pray that this conversation also leads to renewed lives of discipleship. Good theology always leads the church to God and sets the church on mission. Therefore, our prayer is that this conversation will encourage those in the Stone-Campbell movement and all people to examine their theological commitments, submit them to God, and follow God's call into deeper worship and greater service in the kingdom.

FURTHER READING

Allen, C. Leonard. *Things Unseen: Churches of Christ In (and After) the Modern Age.* Siloam Springs, AR: Leafwood Publishers, 2004.

Foster, Douglas A. *The Story of Churches of Christ.* Abilene, TX: Abilene Christian University Press, 2013.

Hughes, Richard T. *Reviving the Ancient Faith: The Story of Churches of Christ in America.* Grand Rapids, MI: Eerdmans, 1996.

Williams, D. Newell, Douglas A. Foster, and Paul M. Blowers, eds. *The Stone-Campbell Movement: A Global History.* St. Louis: Chalice, 2013.

Chapter Two

STARTING WITH GOD: THE TRINITY

A religion not honoring God the Father of all—not relying upon the person, mission, death of the WORD INCARNATE—not inspired, cherished, animated, and inflamed by the Holy Spirit dwelling in my soul, is a cheat, a base counterfeit.

—Alexander Campbell (1841)

Discipleship occurs in community, first and foremost, as Christians participate in the divine community of the Father, Son, and Holy Spirit.

Christian theology and discipleship begin and end with God, or more specifically the Christian understanding of God as Father, Son, and Holy Spirit. Without a clear understanding of who God is and what God is doing, any theological vision is subject to false starts, misplaced emphases, and a failure to benefit from the riches of Christian thought and practice. The Trinity is important for discipleship because without an emphasis on God and God's action, discipleship easily becomes human-centered and works-oriented.

Early Stone-Campbell leaders, who rejected all creeds and abstract theological reflection in favor of a simple, biblical faith, debated the importance of traditional Trinitarian beliefs and formulations. Today, many conservative heirs of the movement share this same hesitancy toward Trinitarian doctrine and language, though most of these heirs hold an implicit Trinitarian view. Nonetheless, numerous early leaders in the Stone-Campbell movement recognized the centrality of a Trinitarian vision of God for Christian thought and discipleship.[1] The Stone-Campbell restoration plea and Christian discipleship are best conceived and receive their proper emphasis when one starts with the one God who is Father, Son, and Holy Spirit.

This chapter begins by presenting the Trinitarian views of two namesakes of the movement: Barton W. Stone and Alexander Campbell. Then a case for Trinitarian doctrine is made by appealing to Scripture and patristic authors, who lived in the first few centuries after the writing of the New Testament. The chapter closes with reflections on the significance of a Trinitarian vision of God for Christian discipleship, as well as suggestions for incorporating Trinitarian doctrine in the life of the church.

THE TRINITY IN THE STONE-CAMPBELL MOVEMENT

The Trinitarian debates of the fourth century generated a number of technical terms and formulas, but the key issues surrounding the doctrine of the Trinity are easily summarized. Trinitarian doctrine upholds the unity, diversity, and full divinity of the Father, Son, and Holy Spirit. In other words, Trinitarian thought maintains belief

---

[1] In addition to Alexander Campbell, other historic Stone-Campbell leaders who advocate a Trinitarian vision of God, some of whom reject Trinitarian language as being non-biblical, include Thomas Campbell, Isaac Errett, Robert Milligan, and David Lipscomb. See Kelly Carter, *The Trinity in the Stone-Campbell Movement: Restoring the Heart of Christian Faith* (Abilene, TX: Abilene Christian University Press, 2015), 29–46; Isaac Errett, *Our Position* (Cincinnati: Standard Publishing, 1873), chapters 1–2; Robert Milligan, *The Scheme of Redemption* (Nashville: Gospel Advocate Company, 2001), 18–23; and David Lipscomb, *Salvation from Sin*, ed. J. W. Shepherd (Nashville: Gospel Advocate Company, 1950), 26–108.

in one God (unity), not three or numerous other gods. Trinitarian doctrine maintains real distinctions between the Father, Son, and Holy Spirit (diversity), and avoids any attempt to blur or erase these distinctions. The Father is not the Son nor the Spirit, the Son is not the Father nor the Spirit, and the Spirit is not the Father nor the Son. Trinitarian thought maintains the eternality and equal divinity of the Father, Son, and Holy Spirit (full divinity), and avoids any attempt to qualify or deny the divinity of the Son and the Spirit. Whatever the Son and the Spirit do in the creation and redemption of all things is what God (and not some other) does.

Trinitarian doctrine, therefore, presents a dynamic understanding of the one God that includes real diversity and community within the Godhead. God the Father consistently works through the Son and by the power of the Holy Spirit. Later in the fifth century, early Christians also affirmed that in the incarnation, the Son truly became a human being, just like us, in Jesus of Nazareth. These beliefs—that the one God is Father, Son, and Holy Spirit, and that Jesus is fully human and fully divine—are so foundational that to deny them is to place oneself outside the boundaries of historic Christian belief.

Nonetheless, Trinitarian thought raises a number of difficult questions and has always had detractors. In the seventeenth and eighteenth centuries during the rise of modernity in the West, Trinitarian critics rejected the doctrine as being unnecessarily mysterious and even contrary to reason. Further, these critics argued that Greek philosophy influenced Trinitarian thought and distorted the simple teachings of Jesus and the early Christians. The rejection of Trinitarian thought often included a skepticism about Jesus's divine identity and a rejection of God's ongoing work in the world through the Spirit. Modern critics of the Trinity viewed Jesus as an exceptional Jewish rabbi who encouraged his followers to love God and live morally, but not as the eternal Son of God who became human. These same critics often embraced a Deistic view that allowed for a creator God, but one who is now far removed from ongoing events in the world. The Holy Spirit and God's ongoing activity in the world were either rejected outright or quietly ignored. The Stone-Campbell movement emerged within this modern backdrop, and its early leaders, though more conservative than some of the Enlightenment critics, shared the modern hesitancy toward the Trinity and religious mystery.

Barton W. Stone, one of the namesakes of the Stone-Campbell movement, rejected Trinitarian belief outright. When Stone pursued ordination in the Transylvania Presbytery of Kentucky, he privately shared his concerns with his ordination examiners. Stone's examiners, who shared his misgivings on the Trinity, encouraged him to proceed and helped him navigate the ordination process. When asked if he accepted the Westminster Confession of Faith, which includes an affirmation of the Trinity, he responded, "I do, as far as I see it consistent with the word of God."[2] Stone questioned Trinitarian doctrine because he saw it to be inconsistent with both the teaching of Scripture and reason.

Stone's presentation of the Trinity is found in several places, and he was widely criticized for his views. In the second edition of *An Address to the Christian Churches in Kentucky, Tennessee, and Ohio*, Stone responds to these criticisms and further clarifies his views. In the introduction, Stone begins with the admonition to "[t]ry every doctrine by the Bible, the only infallible standard."[3] Stone then proceeds to reject the doctrine of the Trinity in favor of

---

[2] Barton W. Stone, "A Short History of the Life of Barton W. Stone, Written by Himself," in *The Biography of Elder Barton Warren Stone, Written by Himself: with Additions and Reflections*, ed. John Rogers (Cincinnati: J. A. & U. P. James, 1847), 29–30.

[3] Barton W. Stone, *An Address to the Christian Churches in Kentucky, Tennessee, and Ohio on Several Important Doctrines of Religion*, 2nd ed. (Lexington: I. T. Cavins & Co., 1821), iii.

a strict monotheism. His discussion of the Son of God in section 2 is particularly revealing:

> There are three general opinions respecting the Son of God. One is, That he is the eternal Son of God—eternally begotten of the Father. Another is, that the Son of God never existed until he was born of Mary 1820 years ago. The third is that the Son of God did not begin to exist 1820 years ago; nor was he eternally begotten; but that he was the first begotten of the Father, the first born of every creature; brought forth before all worlds; and in the fullness of time was united with a body prepared for him; and in whom dwelt all the fullness of Godhead bodily. This last option I profess to be mine.[4]

Stone clearly rejects the Trinitarian view, represented in the first position he presents, in favor of an alternative view that he presents last. For Stone, the Son of God is neither eternal nor fully divine but is subordinate in being to the Father—the only true God. When the Son becomes a human being, all the fullness of God dwells within the man Jesus, but Jesus is not God incarnate.[5]

Stone clarifies the staggering implications of his views as he continues to argue against Trinitarian doctrine:

> With the notion of the Son being very and eternal God, let us turn to Bethlehem, and humbly ask; Who is he that was born of the Virgin Mary! Our brethren . . . say that the second person of the trinity, very and eternal

---

[4] Stone, *An Address*, 13.
[5] A more detailed view of Stone's position is presented in Carter, *The Trinity in the Stone-Campbell Movement*, chapter 3, especially pp. 113–14. Carter labels Stone's view as "*Quasi-Arian*." Stone did not believe the Son was "created *ex nihilo*" from the Father but was "derived" from the Father in time and united to a preexistent, created human soul.

God took man's nature in the womb of the virgin, and of her was born. Is it possible that our brethren believe that the very and only true God, was born of Mary?[6]

He quickly discards what Christians through history have unequivocally confessed: that God, and in particular the Son of God, truly became human in Jesus of Nazareth.

Stone then turns to the cross:

Let us turn to the cross and ask, who is he that suffers, bleeds and dies? The articles before quoted say, That the second person of the trinity was united with our nature, that the two whole and entire natures, Godhead and manhood, were *inseparably* united, *never to be divided*, very God and very man in one person, who truly suffered, was crucified, dead and buried [sic], to reconcile the Father to us.[7]

Again, Stone finds absurd what Christians have historically embraced: that it is God, and not some other, who dies on the cross for the redemption of all things. Stone's doctrine of the Spirit does not fare any better, as Stone viewed the Spirit as God's impersonal power, not God's personal presence.[8]

Much more is at stake here than the splitting of theological hairs. At stake in Trinitarian doctrine is the very narrative and logic of the Christian faith. Fortunately, Stone's views on the Trinity had only marginal sway on the movement, and it was Alexander Campbell, who opposed the non-Trinitarian views of Stone and the Unitarians, who exercised the greatest influence.

---

[6] Stone, *An Address*, 15.
[7] Stone, *An Address*, 16.
[8] Carter, *The Trinity in the Stone-Campbell Movement*, 131–32.

Alexander Campbell, however, had his own misgivings regarding Trinitarian doctrine. Campbell rejected the word *Trinity*, since it does not appear in the New Testament; wanted to avoid abstract theological speculation; and sought to use only biblical language when describing the Godhead. Nonetheless, in his correspondence with Stone and the Unitarians, he presented a position that is essentially Trinitarian and even used traditional, non-biblical terms like *triune, essence,* and *persons.* No matter how hard he tried, Campbell could not avoid Trinitarian speculation when he addressed the shortcomings of the positions of Stone and the Unitarians. Campbell's Disciples of Christ and Stone's Christians united in 1832, but only on the condition that Stone cease theological speculation and commit to using only biblical words. Stone and Campbell could agree that Jesus is "Lord," "Son of God," and "Messiah," but they held radically different conceptions of what these titles imply. For Campbell, these titles implied the full divinity of Jesus, but for Stone, they did not. The differences between Campbell and Stone inevitably appeared in other discussions—most notably in their disagreement on the atonement.[9]

In 1839, Campbell published *The Christian System*, which is in large part a reprint of his 1836 work *Christianity Restored*.[10] The one significant difference in the two works is that *The Christian System* opens with a different essay, also called "The Christian System," which begins with a brief summary of principles for interpreting Scripture (chapter 2) and then proceeds to an articulation of the doctrine of God (chapters 3–5) that was missing altogether in *Christianity Restored*. This presentation of the Father, Son, and

---

[9] See John Mark Hicks, "What Did Christ Accomplish on the Cross? Atonement in Campbell, Stone, and Scott," *Lexington Theological Quarterly* 30, no. 3 (1995): 145–70.

[10] Alexander Campbell, *Christianity Restored* (Bethany, VA: M'Vey and Ewing, 1835), and *The Christian System*, 2nd ed. (Pittsburg, PA: Forrester & Campbell, 1839; repr. Nashville: Gospel Advocate, 1970).

Holy Spirit was undoubtedly motivated by the persistent criticism of his association with Stone and the influence of the Unitarians among the Disciples and Christians.

The Christian System illustrates well Campbell's mature position on the doctrine of God. Campbell states, "Hence we have the Father, Son, and Holy Spirit equally divine, though personally distinct from each other. We have, in fact, but one God, one Lord, one Holy Spirit; yet these are equally possessed of one and the same divine nature." Campbell proposes that God should be conceived not as a "mathematical unit," but as "having plurality, relation, and society in himself."[11] Interestingly, Campbell differs from historic Trinitarian thought in that he reserves the title "Son" for the relationship between the Father and the second person of the Godhead after the incarnation; and following John's Gospel, he uses "Word of God" for the second person of the Godhead before the incarnation. Campbell makes this distinction, though, to secure the full divinity of the second person of the Trinity, worrying that the title "Son" denigrates the second person of the Godhead when used indiscriminately. For Campbell, the Father/Son relation begins after the incarnation.[12] Campbell holds that "the phrase 'the Word of God' denotes an eternal, unoriginated relation," and he clearly views the second person of the Trinity as fully divine.[13]

Further, Campbell affirms the personality of the Holy Spirit, noting that the Spirit is "not an impersonal power, but a living, energizing, active, personal existence. Hence in all the works of God the Spirit of God is the active, operating agent."[14] He continues, "The Spirit is said to do, and to have done, all that God

---

[11] Campbell, *The Christian System*, 8.
[12] Carter discusses Campbell's distinction between the "Word" and "Son" more fully in *The Trinity and the Stone-Campbell Movement*, 51–54.
[13] Campbell, *The Christian System*, 10.
[14] Campbell, *The Christian System*, 11.

does and all that God has done."[15] When discussing the church, Campbell notes that "Jesus is the *head*, and the Spirit is the *life* and animating principle of that body."[16] Campbell closes his initial discussion of the Father, Son, and Spirit with these emphatic words:

> The divine doctrine of these holy and incomprehensible relations in the Divinity is so inwrought and incorporated with all the parts of the sacred book—so identified with all the dispensations of religion—and so essential to the mediatorship of Christ, that it is impossible to make any real and divine proficiency in the true knowledge of God, of man, of reconciliation, of remission of sins, of eternal life, or in the piety and divine life of Christ's religion, without a clear and distinct perception of it, as well as a firm and unshaken faith and confidence in it, as we trust still to make more evident in the sequel.[17]

Another fascinating section of Campbell's *The Christian System* is his "Summary View of the Christian System of Facts" (see Appendix Two).[18] Campbell's "Summary" has numerous similarities in content to the baptismal confessions, rules of faith, and creeds of the church of the first four centuries (see Appendix One). And like many of these early Christian confessions, Campbell's "Summary" is organized around the three divine persons God/Father, Word/Son, and the Holy Spirit. Despite his misgivings over the word *Trinity* and his attempt to avoid abstract theological speculation, Campbell follows the primary concerns of the early Christians who formulated Trinitarian beliefs in both his presentation of the Godhead and his summary of Christian belief.

---

[15] Campbell, *The Christian System*, 11.
[16] Campbell, *The Christian System*, 11.
[17] Campbell, *The Christian System*, 11.
[18] Campbell, *The Christian System*, 54–55.

THE TRINITY IN THE EARLY CHURCH

The early church invested significant energy in clarifying its doctrine of God and in particular its understanding of Jesus. The development of Trinitarian doctrine ran parallel to, and received more formal attention and debate than, the canonization of the twenty-seven books of the New Testament. Of course, interesting questions naturally emerge regarding the Father, Son, and Holy Spirit: How can the one God also be three distinct "persons," and how can Jesus be fully divine and fully human? These concepts appear to be contradictory. But more was at stake in the formulation of Trinitarian doctrine than tackling intellectual curiosities. At stake was the Christian understanding of God in a pluralistic context and the very narrative of the Christian faith. The early church existed in a context where the word *god* could refer to numerous competing deities and ideologies. The revealed name "Father, Son, and Holy Spirit" was used to call on God in worship and delineate a specifically Christian understanding of God in a pluralistic environment. Further, the early church professed that God, and in particular the Son of God, really became human and lived among us as the man Jesus of Nazareth. When the Son became human, though, God did not cease to sustain creation and answer prayers, including the prayers of Jesus. When Jesus died on the cross, God truly died for us, and yet, God the Father raised Jesus by the Spirit's power. When the resurrected Jesus poured out the Holy Spirit on the church, God did not cease to be transcendent and sustain all creation, and yet, through the Spirit, God intimately dwells within the church as a whole and Christians individually. In baptism, Christians are united to Christ, receive the Holy Spirit, and, as children of God, participate in the divine life and the divine project of redeeming all creation. Nothing less than the very understanding of God and the narrative of the

Christian faith was at stake in the Trinitarian discussions that reached a high point in the fourth and fifth centuries.

The New Testament does not explicitly present Trinitarian doctrine, but neither are the New Testament authors silent on the relevant issues. Various New Testament authors, writing in different locations and times, uphold the oneness of God (Mark 12:29; 1 Cor. 8:4; James 2:19). The full divinity of Jesus is affirmed throughout John's Gospel. In his majestic prologue, John begins, "In the beginning was the Word, and the Word was with God, and the Word was God" (John 1:1). At the end of the Gospel, John records Thomas's testimony, "My Lord and my God!" (John 20:28), which identifies Jesus as God. Paul refers to Jesus as the one who "being in very nature God, did not consider equality with God something to be used to his own advantage" (Phil. 2:6). The author of Hebrews states that Jesus is "the radiance of God's glory and the exact representation of his being, sustaining all things by his powerful word" (Heb. 1:3). Further, the author of Hebrews affirms the full humanity of Jesus, maintaining that Jesus had to be "fully human in every way, in order that he might become a merciful and faithful high priest in service to God, and that he might make atonement for the sins of the people" (Heb. 2:17; see also John 1:14 and Phil. 2:7).

The full divinity of the Spirit is less emphasized, but nevertheless the Spirit is called "holy" and even "eternal" (Heb. 9:14). Christians individually and the church as a whole are called the temple of God because of the indwelling of the Holy Spirit (1 Cor. 3:16–17; 6:19–20; 2 Cor. 6:16), but this image only works if the Spirit is fully divine. The Spirit's work is God's work, and Peter equates lying to the Spirit with lying to God (Acts 5:3–4). The personal nature of the Spirit is evident by the actions, deliberations, and emotions that the New Testament authors attribute to the Spirit. The Spirit "searches all things, even the deep things of God"

(1 Cor. 2:10); distributes spiritual gifts to Christians, "just as he determines" (1 Cor. 12:11); grieves when Christians sin (Eph. 4:30); teaches (John 14:26); hears (John 16:13); speaks (Acts 10:19–20); judges (Acts 15:28); witnesses (Rom. 8:16); and intercedes (Rom. 8:27). None of these descriptions are appropriate for an impersonal power but are naturally ascribed to a personal agent.

Trinitarian doctrine receives further support from the numerous biblical passages that join God, God's word, and God's spirit in the Old Testament (for example, Gen. 1:1–3; Ps. 33:6; Ezek. 37:1–10), and the Father, Son, and Holy Spirit in the New Testament. In the Ephesian letter alone, Trinitarian patterns of Father, Son, and Holy Spirit appear in 1:3–14 (which is one sentence in the original Greek), 1:17, 2:18, 2:22, 3:4–5, 3:16–17, 4:3–6, and 5:18–20. Paul closes 2 Corinthians with a Trinitarian benediction: "May the grace of the Lord Jesus Christ, and the love of God, and the fellowship of the Holy Spirit be with you all" (2 Cor. 13:14). In the Great Commission, Jesus instructs his followers to baptize "in the name of the Father and of the Son and of the Holy Spirit" (Matt. 28:19). These last two examples are especially significant because they involve settings of worship—that is, a closing prayer of blessing and the Christian initiation rite.

After the writing of the New Testament, the early church followed this same Trinitarian usage as they worshiped, prayed, baptized, and passed on the essential elements of the faith through evangelism and instruction. *The Apostolic Tradition* (ca. 215) records a baptismal creed that converts affirmed at their baptism. The creed has three articles structured around the Father, Son, and Holy Spirit, and converts were immersed three times—one each for the Father, Son, and Holy Spirit (see Appendix One). Baptismal creeds like this were influenced by Jesus's words in the Great Commission to baptize "in the name of the Father and of the Son and of the Holy Spirit" (Matt. 28:19).

The various rules of faith that appear in the second and third centuries include similar Trinitarian structure and content. The rules of faith were summaries of Christian belief that, although similar in content, varied in wording and therefore were less fixed than formal creedal statements. Some of these rules are structured around Father and Son only, but more often, they are structured around Father, Son, and Holy Spirit. In *Proof of the Apostolic Preaching* (ca. 180–200), Irenaeus of Lyons presents a rule of faith that is explicitly structured around the three "headings" of Father, Son, and Holy Spirit (see Appendix One).

Trinitarian doctrine receives its classic formulation in the Nicene Creed, which is traditionally attributed to the Second Ecumenical Council at Constantinople (381 AD). The Nicene Creed follows the Trinitarian structure of earlier baptismal creeds and rules of faith, emphasizes the full divinity of the Son, and affirms the appropriateness of worshiping the Holy Spirit along with the Father and the Son (see Appendix One). Regarding this last point, just as it is appropriate to baptize "in the name of the Father and of the Son and of the Holy Spirit," so is it appropriate to worship Father, Son, and Holy Spirit. As in the early-eighteenth-century hymn "Doxology," the phrases "Praise God from whom all blessings flow" and "Praise Father, Son, and Holy Ghost" are considered equivalent.

In addition to clarifying significant issues regarding the identity of the Son and the Spirit, the Nicene Creed provides a summary of basic Christian belief that is useful for evangelism and teaching. Besides being structured around the Trinitarian vision of God as Father, Son, and Holy Spirit, the creed also addresses the following topics: creation; the incarnation, crucifixion, resurrection, coronation, and second coming of Jesus; divine revelation and Scripture; the church; baptism for the forgiveness of sins; and the resurrection of the dead and eternal life. The Nicene Creed is the most widely affirmed statement of Christian belief through history and offers the church today a concrete, historical statement of basic Christian belief.

The Trinitarian vision of God was clearly important to the early church, as evident in its baptismal creeds, rules of faith, and formal creedal statements, and this vision emerged from a careful reading of Scripture. In his groundbreaking work on early creeds, including confessional statements in the New Testament, J. N. D. Kelly argues:

> The Trinitarianism of the New Testament is rarely explicit; but the frequency with which the triadic schema recurs . . . suggests that this pattern was implicit in Christian theology from the start. If these gaps are filled in, however, we are entitled to assume with some confidence that what we have before us, at any rate in rough outline, is the doctrinal deposit, or the pattern of sound words, which was expounded in the apostolic Church since its inauguration and which constituted its distinctive message.[19]

In other words, it is not difficult to draw a line from the implicit Trinitarian statements of the New Testament to the explicit Trinitarian statements of the early church. But Trinitarian reflection, whether for the early church or today, is not simply about doctrinal correctness, as important as this is. The revelation of God as Father, Son, and Holy Spirit inevitably impacts Christian discipleship. Trinitarian reflection, both old and new, should carefully consider how Trinitarian doctrine shapes the entirety of Christian theology and impacts Christians' living and practice.

---

[19] J. N. D. Kelly, *Early Christian Creeds*, 3rd ed. (London: Longman, 1972), 12–13.

THE TRINITY AND DISCIPLESHIP

From the beginning, early Stone-Campbell leaders were interested in restoring New Testament beliefs and practices for the sake of doctrinal faithfulness, Christian unity, the mission of the church, and freedom of conscience. Rather than take away from these core concerns, as early Stone-Campbell leaders worried, Trinitarian doctrine actually helps strengthen these concerns and, as we hope to make evident in subsequent chapters, other doctrinal commitments of Churches of Christ.

Trinitarian doctrine provides a concrete, historical vision of God, including the identity of Jesus, which is foundational for Christian belief. Alexander Campbell increasingly saw the importance of a specific understanding of God as Father, Son, and Holy Spirit, and a specific understanding of Jesus as both fully divine and fully human, that a strict commitment to biblical language and a vague understanding of Jesus did not secure. Stone and the Unitarians could confess that Jesus is "Lord," "Son of God," and "Messiah," yet still deny the full divinity of the Son and the Spirit. A commitment to Trinitarian doctrine helps secure a commitment to biblical and historic Christian belief.

A commitment to Trinitarian doctrine provides a basis for Christian unity. Throughout its history, the Stone-Campbell movement has wavered between an ecumenical vision that is either too broad, as seen in the writings of Stone, or too narrow, as seen in sectarian visions that insist others adopt Stone-Campbell doctrinal emphases and practices. Trinitarian doctrine provides a specific vision of God and an interpretive lens for reading the biblical narrative that, historically and today, a large majority of Christians either explicitly or implicitly affirms. And yet, clearly, a confessional unity around a Trinitarian vision of God still allows for significant disagreements and tensions. Trinitarian doctrine is consistent with and even strengthens Stone-Campbell emphases and practices, and at the same time helps Stone-Campbell heirs hold these emphases and practices with a healthier perspective. Further, Trinitarian doctrine preserves the theological category of mystery. God is holy and other, and there are some things we simply cannot know about God this side of eternity and beyond. A Trinitarian vision of God helps Christians balance doctrinal faithfulness, Christian unity, and freedom of conscience.

Trinitarian doctrine can help Stone-Campbell heirs develop a healthier view of the Holy Spirit. Historically, Stone-Campbell representatives have emphasized Scripture and the past over the ongoing work of God in the present, primarily due to a concern that the present "leading of the Spirit" is too subjective. This concern about the subjective nature of the Spirit's work has led to a near conflation of Scripture and the Spirit. For instance, Alexander Campbell emphasized that the Spirit of God works through the preaching of the Word, especially in conversion.[20] This observation is true, but it is also misleading if one insists that the Spirit works *only* through the preaching of the Word.

God has truly revealed God's character, will, and purposes in the past, especially in the life and teachings of Jesus, the incarnate Son. Christians must carefully attend to this past deposit of the faith. At the same time, God continues to work in the world today through the Holy Spirit. The leading of the Spirit is not confined to the words of Scripture, but God's Spirit will not lead us away from the revelation of God in Jesus Christ. A Trinitarian vision of God helps Christians maintain a balance between the past work of God through the Son as recorded in Scripture and the ongoing leading of the Spirit in the present.

---

[20] For a presentation and critical discussion of Campbell's view of the Spirit in conversion, see Robert C. Kurka, "The Role of the Holy Spirit in Conversion: Why Restorationists Appear to Be Out of the Evangelical Mainstream," in *Evangelicalism and the Stone-Campbell Movement*, ed. William R. Baker (Downers Grove, IL: InterVarsity Press Books, 2002), ch. 6.

Trinitarian doctrine emphasizes the priority of divine action over human action. Throughout the New Testament a pattern emerges in which God the Father continually comes to humanity through the Son and by the power of the Spirit, and draws humanity to the Father by the Spirit's power through the mediating work of the Son. In other words, humans exist in the middle of the dynamic action of God so that humans might share in the life and reign of God. We do not have to wonder or guess at the character of God because God is graciously revealed to us through the Son and by the Spirit's power. Further, when Scripture is read and proclaimed, the Spirit convicts and encourages all people, but especially Christians in whom the Spirit dwells. Salvation is not based on human efforts but is a gift the Father graciously gives through the redeeming work of the Son. If we are in Christ, then Jesus's righteousness is our righteousness, Jesus's holiness is our holiness, and Jesus's sonship is ours by adoption. At the same time, the Spirit works in us and with us to perfect us in holiness and the "fruit of the Spirit" (Gal. 5:22–23).

The priority of divine action over human action is also crucial for the church's participation in God's mission. Christian mission is not the product of human wisdom, nor is it accomplished by human power. Rather, Christians participate in Jesus's ongoing ministry in the world—this is God's work, not our work. Furthermore, Christians are empowered by the same Spirit who empowered Jesus in his mission. The church today glorifies the Father by participating in the ongoing mission of Jesus by the power of the Spirit.

Birthed in the American context, the Stone-Campbell movement has typically emphasized human initiative in conversion, growth in holiness, and mission. At one level, this is appropriate, as God does cooperate with humans to bring about God's purposes in creation. But if the priority and utter necessity of divine grace and divine action is missed, then Christian living becomes a human-centered and works-oriented affair. A Trinitarian vision of God emphasizes divine action and divine grace. God has not left the church alone in this world.

Trinitarian doctrine highlights the communal and relational nature of human existence. The one God is also the perfect divine community of the Trinity. Before creation, God was not lonely or in need of companionship, but instead exists eternally as the Father, Son, and Holy Spirit. God created humans as relational beings, created in the image of God, to share in the divine community, but sin destroys our communion with God and each other. Nonetheless, the Father is restoring our fellowship with God and each other through Christ and by the Spirit's power. In baptism, Christians are united with Christ, receive the indwelling of the Spirit, and become part of God's redeemed people, the church. Jesus summarizes the Christian life with two relational commands: love God and love others (Matt. 22:36–40). Human existence and Christian salvation are deeply relational, and this relationality comes from the nature of the Triune God.

Christian ethics and living flow out of the nature and work of the Trinitarian God. Christian virtues like love, humility, and generosity can be vague concepts, but New Testament authors point to the incarnation and crucifixion of God's Son to provide a concrete example of virtue in action. Consider how John defines love: "This is love: not that we loved God, but that he loved us and sent his Son as an atoning sacrifice for our sins" (1 John 4:10). For John, the Son is not a created being—no matter how highly exalted—who becomes human and dies for us. The Father does not send a third party for our salvation. Rather, it is God the Son who becomes human and dies for us. What the Son does is what God does for us. The implication for our lives is clear: "Dear friends, since God so loved us, we also ought to love one another" (1 John 4:11). We are to love as God loves. Christian love flows out of the nature and action of God on our behalf.

Such a high understanding of love, however, goes beyond natural human inclinations. We have a difficult time loving our friends, not to speak of our enemies. So how is such a life of love possible? The biblical authors stress that a life of love is only possible because of the Holy Spirit's work in us. It is the Spirit who helps us grow in love and Christlikeness (Gal. 5:22–23; 1 Cor. 13).

Throughout his writings, Paul repeatedly calls Christians to imitate the nature and actions of God. For instance, Paul calls the Philippian church to a life of humility by pointing to the incarnation and crucifixion of Jesus (Phil. 2). Paul challenges the Corinthian church to grow in generosity by pointing to the example of Jesus (2 Cor. 8:9). But as with John, the example of Jesus is not the example of a third party standing between God and humans; the example of Jesus is the example of God on our behalf. It is God the Son who humbled himself for us, and it is God the Son who was so generous to us. God is characterized by and acts in humility and generosity, and so Christians should strive to be humble and generous as well. Further, it is God, and in particular the Spirit, who helps Christians "to will and to act in order to fulfill [God's] good purpose" (Phil. 2:12–13) and grow in the "grace" of generosity (2 Cor. 8:1).

INCORPORATING TRINITARIAN DOCTRINE IN THE LIFE OF THE CHURCH

Given the historical significance and wide acceptance of the Nicene Creed, some Christian traditions recite the creed in worship as a confession of the historic Christian faith and a symbol of unity. Despite our reluctance toward creeds, Churches of Christ should consider adopting this practice. When Christians recite the Nicene Creed before the Lord's Supper, Christians proclaim in words and symbolic actions our commitment to the historic Christian faith and the unity of the church.[21]

The Nicene Creed is an outline of foundational Christian beliefs, and churches could use the creed either explicitly or indirectly for teaching new converts and even mature Christians. The Nicene Creed addresses (1) God as Trinity, (2) creation, (3) the incarnation of Jesus, (4) the crucifixion of Jesus, (5) the resurrection of Jesus, (6) the ascension and coronation of Jesus, (7) the second coming of Jesus, (8) the Holy Spirit, (9) divine revelation and Scripture, (10) the church, (11) baptism for the forgiveness of sins, and (12) the resurrection of the dead and eternal life.

There is hesitancy toward reciting creeds in Churches of Christ, but we have always sung our confessions of faith. There are numerous songs, both old and new, that directly affirm Trinitarian doctrine. The verses of some of these songs are structured around Father, Son, and Holy Spirit, much like the early rules of faith and creeds. Churches should sing Trinitarian songs more regularly and intentionally.

In preaching and Bible study, we could intentionally highlight and reflect on Trinitarian patterns, as well as the emphases on divine action, that appear throughout the New Testament (for instance, in 1 Cor. 12:4–6, 1 Pet. 1:2, and Rom. 8, to list just a few).

Prayers are Trinitarian in that we can only come into the presence of a holy God through the mediating work of Jesus (or "in Jesus's name") and by the Spirit's power (Rom. 8:26). We should ask the Father, in Jesus's name, for the Spirit to lead and empower the church and to give us wisdom (Acts 4:24–31). Prayer can also reflect the priority of divine action over human action when it includes times of silence, listening for God, and waiting on God.

---

[21] See Mark E. Powell, "Proclaiming the Gospel at the Table," in *Christian Studies* 30 (2018): 95–104, especially pp. 98–101.

Worship services could include Trinitarian benedictions, such as reciting 2 Cor. 13:14 or singing the Doxology. More could be said about the significance of a Trinitarian vision of God. These observations, however, give some sense of the promise of starting Stone-Campbell theological reflection—and all Christian theological reflection—with the one God who is Father, Son, and Holy Spirit. In doing so, Stone-Campbell heirs and Churches of Christ in particular follow the early church more closely in their reading of Scripture, understanding of unity, and practice of discipleship.

FURTHER READING

Carter, Kelly D. *The Trinity in the Stone-Campbell Movement: Recovering the Heart of the Christian Faith*. Abilene, TX: Abilene Christian University Press, 2014.

Fairbairn, Donald. *Life in the Trinity: An Introduction to Theology with the Help of the Church Fathers*. Downers Grove, IL: InterVarsity Press Academic, 2009.

Powell, Mark E. *Centered in God: The Trinity and Christian Spirituality*. Abilene, TX: Abilene Christian University Press, 2014.

Sanders, Fred. *The Deep Things of God: How the Trinity Changes Everything*, 2nd ed. Wheaton, IL: Crossway, 2017.

Chapter Three

PARTICIPATING IN GOD'S STORY: ESCHATOLOGY

I have observed that those speakers as a rule secure the greatest number of accessions who dwell most upon escaping hell and getting into heaven, and least upon the importance of leading lives of absolute consecration to the Lord; in other words their converts are much more anxious to be saved than they are to follow Christ.

—James A. Harding (1887)

Eschatology, the study of "last things," is not so much about what happens last—or the order in which it happens—as much as it is about the future that is already at work, how this rescues humanity both now and in the future, and how it places a call on our lives as followers of Jesus in the present. Disciples are committed to following Jesus rather than "escaping hell and going to heaven."

Eschatology is the whole story of Scripture—the story of salvation from creation to new creation. As John Chryssavgis put it, "Eschatology is not a teaching about the last things after everything else but rather the teaching about the relation of all things to the

47

last things, in essence the *last-ness* and *lasting-ness* of things."[1] It is the story of how creation gives birth to new creation and the "lasting-ness" of creation through union with God, which is God's goal for the creation.

Discipleship, rather than obsessing about the order in which the last things will happen or what prophetic events appear on the horizon, focuses on experiencing the already-present future and participating in the mission of God embodied in the ministry of Jesus as the means by which God brings the future into the present. Disciples pray, "your kingdom come, your will be done, on earth as it is in heaven" (Matt. 6:10).

ESCHATOLOGY IN THE STONE-CAMPBELL MOVEMENT

The Stone-Campbell movement's origins are deeply rooted in eschatological hopes. The optimism of the new American nation nurtured postmillennialism in the nineteenth century. Alexander Campbell, Walter Scott, and Robert Milligan embraced this vision—God is at work to bring peace and justice to the whole world through the historical triumph of Christianity. Others, such as Barton W. Stone, David Lipscomb, and James A. Harding, adopted an apocalyptic understanding of history, which often included historic premillennialism. They expected God to fully realize the hopes of God's rule over the cosmos only when Christ personally returned to earth to reign over creation. Both streams expected God to renew the earth and reign with the saints in a new creation.

Their discipleship was shaped and compelled by that vision. Their eschatological hopes imbued disciples with a spirit of obedience as a way of hastening the coming of the kingdom's fullness. For example, every person who heeds "the voice of Jesus" and

---

[1] John Chryssavgis, *Beyond the Shattered Image* (Minneapolis: Light and Life Publishing, 1999), 34.

strives "to follow Christ," according to Harding, is "hastening the day when the meek—that is, the humble, mild, gentle, peaceable—shall inherit the earth."[2]

At the heart of this vision is the movement from creation to new creation through regeneration or renewal. Their eschatology is the story of creation, fall, and redemption that culminates in the new heaven and new earth, which is the renovation rather than the annihilation of the creation. God's goal, though detoured by human sin, is the transfiguration of creation itself so that humanity coreigns with God. Soteriology (salvation) serves eschatology (the goal). Given humanity's sin, God rescues the creation through the union of God and humanity. Despite human evil, the Father saves through the Son in the power of the Holy Spirit.

Alexander Campbell

Campbell's 1833 *Millennial Harbinger Extra* (reprinted in *The Christian System*), entitled "Regeneration," quoted Revelation 21:5 on its masthead: "Behold, I make all things new."

The movement from creation to new creation is a progressive one; it moves from good to better. "It is great," Campbell wrote, "to create man in the image of God—greater to redeem his soul from general corruption; but greatest of all to give his mortal frame incorruptible and immortal vigor."[3] God's story began with creation but always intended to give humanity an immortal body within an eternal creation where God, humanity, and the creation would share life together forever.

Divine love is the prime mover. "The universe is, itself, the offspring of God's love."[4] The "grand principle" that grounds both

---

[2] James A. Harding, "Peace, Unity," *The Way* 1, no. 6 (June 5, 1899): 82.

[3] Alexander Campbell, *The Christian System*, 2nd ed. (Pittsburg: Forrester & Campbell, 1839; repr. Nashville: Gospel Advocate, 1970), 235.

[4] Alexander Campbell, *Familiar Lectures on the Pentateuch* (repr. Rosemead, CA: Old Paths Book Club, 1958), 273.

the creative and regenerative work of God is the "sublime proposition" that "GOD IS LOVE," and "it is in the person and mission of the INCARNATE WORD that we learn that *God is love.*" Because of human sin, the Word became flesh for the "renovation of human nature" as well as the whole of creation.[5]

The Father created human nature in the image of God and now regenerates it through the Holy Spirit, who is "as necessary to *the new life,* as the atmosphere is to our" natural existence. With this *personal* new birth, "the Holy Spirit is shed on us richly through Jesus Christ our Saviour; of which the peace of mind, the love, the joy, and the hope of the regenerate is full proof." Indeed, love is the fundamental "rule by which [faith] operates," and "every pulsation of the new heart is the impulse of the spirit of love" through the work of the Spirit.[6] This leads to the transformation of heart and character, "which is the tendency and the fruit of the process of regeneration" (progressive sanctification).[7] And this process is also *communal*—the "regeneration of the church." As the church "progress[es] toward the ancient order," the community of God will embody the life of God in "justice, truth, fidelity, [and] honesty" as it "communes" with God in daily "piety."[8] Discipleship, then, is both personal and communal, and this will ultimately bring the "transformation of the world" as a social reality.[9]

Regeneration is also *cosmic* because the hope of "physical" regeneration is the resurrection of the body. Rather than simply resuscitating us from the dead, Christ promises "to give that raised body the deathless vigor of incorruptibility, to renovate and transform it in all its parts, and to make every spirit feel that it reanimates its own body." The hope of the Christian faith is not

---

[5] Campbell, *The Christian System*, 220-21.
[6] Campbell, *The Christian System*, 234.
[7] Campbell, *The Christian System*, 235.
[8] Campbell, *The Christian System*, 240, 245-46.
[9] Campbell, *The Christian System*, 256.

the immortality of the soul, which is the "doctrine of Plato," but "the immortality of the body" in conformity to Jesus's own resurrection by which he was "made the head of the New Creation."[10]

As that head, Jesus is the head of humanity not merely as the firstborn from the dead but also the firstborn of all creation itself, the heir of all things. Just as the "Bible begins with the generations of the heavens and the earth," Campbell believed, "the Christian revelation ends with the regenerations or new creation of the heavens and the earth." Just as God resurrects the human body, God also "regenerates [the creation], but annihilates nothing."[11]

David Lipscomb

Lipscomb understood the biblical drama through the lens of a conflict between the reign of God and the reign of evil.

In the original creation, the "Spirit of God brooded over it all and impregnated every breath of air with his own life-giving, life-perpetuating, and health-inspiring elixir." The earth itself was the "outer court of the heavenly temple." God entrusted this holy court to divine image bearers. God shared dominion over the creation with them. However, humanity betrayed this trust and transferred its "allegiance and service" to the evil one. As a result, Satan "took up his abode on this earth as the god of this world," as in a "defiled temple," and the earth "became a dried and parched wilderness."[12]

Ever since, God's goal, revealed in "the mission of Christ to earth, was to rescue the world from the rule and dominion of the evil one" and "to rehabilitate it with the dignity and the glory it had when it came from the hand of God."[13] This includes not only

---

[10] Campbell, *The Christian System*, 236.
[11] Campbell, *The Christian System*, 257.
[12] David Lipscomb, *Salvation from Sin*, ed. J. W. Shepherd (Nashville: Gospel Advocate, 1913), 111–12.
[13] Lipscomb, *Salvation from Sin*, 114.

the restoration of humanity to their rule over the creation but the redemption of creation itself.

The divine project is to "restore" humanity—"spiritually, mentally, and physically—to the likeness of its Maker" so that humanity might once again rule in "this rescued and restored kingdom of God." There, God will renew the "beauty of Eden" and "make the desert blossom" like a rose. This "material, moral, and spiritual" goal is comprehensive so that God might fully inhabit the creation as a temple where "God's Spirit must dwell" and divine "blessings and protection abound."[14] While the creation and fall are "the first acts in the drama," the story ends with "restoration and redemption of the faithful in the more than restored paradise of God."[15] Salvation, as a subset of eschatology, is a restoration project. God intends to restore the earth to its original glory and beyond. Soteriology is eschatology.

According to Lipscomb, we participate in the mission of Christ as disciples or followers of Jesus. Indeed, the Sermon on the Mount taught the "essential principles" that "must pervade and control the hearts and lives" of disciples.[16] These teachings intend to "make [people] like God" that they might "dwell with [God]."[17] The spirit of obedience expressed in following Jesus is the path of renewal and restoration as the principles of the kingdom of God subvert the reign of evil in the world through the obedient lives of disciples.

Summary

Though Campbell and Lipscomb differ over whether the reign of God is progressively victorious (a postmillennial triumphalism)

---

[14] Lipscomb, *Salvation from Sin*, 114–15.
[15] Lipscomb, *Salvation from Sin*, 11.
[16] David Lipscomb, *Civil Government: Its Origin, Mission, and Destiny, and the Christian's Relation to It* (Nashville: Gospel Advocate, 1913), 133.
[17] David Lipscomb, *Queries and Answers*, ed. J. W. Shepherd (Nashville: Gospel Advocate, 1918), 384.

or a decisive and final inbreaking into the present (an apocalyptic victory over evil), they share the same eschatological goal. Though creation has fallen into disorder through human sin, God intends to redeem it rather than annihilate it. God will rescue (save) the creation because God loves it. Just as God created the world through the Son in the power of the Spirit, God will recreate it by the same means.

Disciples of Jesus participate in the divine mission toward the renewal of the full image of God in a new humanity. This not only includes a pious character but also a social vision for living under the rule of God as well as embracing an attitude of creation care. Salvation, shaped by this eschatological vision, is not about "getting saved and getting to heaven," but about participating in the reality of the kingdom of God in the present as disciples of Jesus.

ESCHATOLOGY IN THE EARLY CHURCH

While the biblical drama has a discernible shape, there are diverse but legitimate ways to tell the story. It has a fluid but stable character because the narrative is rich and textured. The following renarration reflects that constancy, but it has a particular emphasis. The eschatological goal is union with God, and God dwells within and fills the creation for the sake of that goal. Dwelling and filling are God's missional agenda, so that God might be in all things and all things in God. That mission is enacted through the vocation of human beings who live in God-indwelt communities—whether Eden, Israel, or the Church—*grounded in, shaped by*, and *moving toward* God's goal.

Act One: Creation

God—the Father, through the Son, in the power of the Spirit—created a blessed community among whom God chose to dwell. God rested within this creation in order to enjoy and commune with the beloved community and blessed world. The creation is the temple of God in which God dwells. God does not construct a house out of brick and mortar but out of earth and sky—a cosmic cathedral. God built a "resting place" for God's own self (Isa. 66:1–2).

God placed an image within this temple (Gen. 1:26–28). As images of God, humanity reflects and represents God in the creation. We are God's coworkers or partners, with whom God fills, develops (subdues the remaining chaos), and cares for (rules or shepherds) this good creation. The goal is to fill the earth with the images of God, who reflect God's glory, and partner with God in moving creation toward the enjoyment of God's eternal seventh day rest.

Yet humanity did not embrace this mission. Though invited to participate in it and enjoy God's rest, humanity created a rival story with its own agenda. Humanity assumed divine prerogatives at Babel when it decided to make a name for itself, rather than represent God (Gen. 11:4). The move from Eden to Babel is chaotic, as it fills the earth with violence, oppression, and immorality rather than the glory of God (Gen. 6:11, 13). Instead of partnering with God to subdue the chaos in the creation, humanity created more chaos by pursuing evil.

God, however, did not abandon the goal.

Act Two: Israel

God blessed Abraham in order to bless all peoples. The blessing God pronounced at creation—to be fruitful, multiply, and fill the earth—is renewed in the promise to Abraham, Isaac, and Jacob (Gen. 28:3). What God initiated in creation is continued in Israel, who is the new humanity in a land where Eden would flourish once again if they were obedient (Lev. 26:9).

God graciously initiated a new relationship with humanity through the call of Abraham, grounded that relationship in the redemptive acts of the Exodus, and at Sinai invited Israel to live as the light of God among the nations as a people among whom God dwelt (Isa. 42:6; 51:4). They were called, like Adam and Eve, to embrace their role as royal priests (Exod. 19:5–6). They were God's priests, even mediators, for the nations. God called Israel into a partnership to live redemptively among the peoples in order to illuminate God's intent for creation, draw all peoples to God, and fill the earth with the images of God.

God dwelt with Israel through faithful presence with Abraham, Isaac, and Jacob; then in the Tabernacle from the wilderness to the reign of David; and then in the Temple in Jerusalem, which became God's gracious "resting place" (Ps. 132:14) where God communed with Israel.

As the residence of God's redemptive presence, Israel became a missional community whose obedience would draw the nations to God. God's covenant of love guided their mission as they lived as divine images among the idolatrous nations of the ancient world. The Torah provided the origins and instruction of the covenant, the histories narrated the story of God's redemptive life with Israel, the prophets called the people to embrace covenantal life, and wise sages applied the life of God to Israel's daily life within God's good yet chaotic creation. Israel was God's image within the creation, and they were invested with God's mission.

Yet Israel embraced the ways of the peoples. Shaped by the nations, they adopted a different path. They pursued the cycles of violence, oppression, and injustice that characterized the peoples for whom they were intended as light. Ultimately, their own evil subverted their mission, and God exiled them from the land, just as God had exiled Adam and Eve from Eden.

God's redemptive purposes, however, were not thwarted, nor did God abandon the goal.

Act Three: Messiah

In the wake of Israel's failure, God entered the world in the person of the Logos (Word) who became flesh and dwelt with humanity (John 1:1, 14). As the true image of God, the enfleshed Word, Jesus the Messiah, fully embodied God's intent in creation. He is the true Israel who dwells in the land in order to fill the land with the glory of God (Matt. 4:12–17) by multiplying the images of God in the world through a new birth (John 1:12–13). In Jesus, God renewed Israel and rebirthed humanity in the image of God. The Father sent the Son in the power of the Spirit to reconcile all things, and through the Spirit, the Son affects the Father's goal to redeem all creation.

The Son became flesh by the power of the Spirit in order to unite God and humanity in the person of the Son. The incarnate Son reveals the Father (John 1:18) and demonstrates the love of the Father (1 John 4:9). Through the Son, the Triune God dwells with Israel in the land and reveals the glory of God.

The Father inaugurated the eschatological reign of God through the Son in the power of the Spirit in order to liberate the creation from its bondage. Baptized in water and anointed with the Spirit, the Messiah ministered in the power of the Spirit (Luke 4:14). God's kingdom broke into the world through healing the sick, raising the dead, administering justice for the oppressed, triumphing over the demonic powers, and preaching good news to the poor. The future kingdom of God was present in the ministry of Jesus, which embodied the divine mission for creation as it reversed the consequences of human sin in the world.

God through the Son was crucified in the flesh and offered a sacrifice through the Spirit in order to break the power of sin and evil in the world (Heb. 9:14). The Messiah faithfully pursued the mission of God, even to death. In his death, he proclaimed God's love for humanity, the Son's love for the Father, and triumphed over the powers that executed him. The Son dwelt with humanity in order to suffer for sin (Heb. 9:26), and through that suffering, the Son redeemed humanity from sin (John 1:29).

The Father raised the Son from the dead with the power of the Spirit (Rom. 1:4; 8:11). Jesus the Messiah was made alive in the Spirit in order to set the world right and give the people of God a renewed status before God (Rom. 4:25). The resurrection of Jesus the Messiah as the firstborn from the dead inaugurated new creation (Col. 1:18). Creation is renewed through the resurrection of his body, his resurrection assures our resurrection, and our resurrection entails the resurrection of creation itself (Rom. 8:18–23).

God enthroned the Son in the power of the Spirit at the Father's right hand (Eph. 1:20). As the new human, Jesus the Messiah is the Lord of creation, and the Father gave Jesus all authority in heaven and on the earth in order to place every power under the rule of God (1 Pet. 3:22) and renew the creation by filling "all the universe" (Eph. 4:10).

Act Four: Church

The Father, through the Son, sent the Spirit to dwell in the body of Christ, which is the presence of Jesus in the world, who fills all things (Eph. 1:23).

Through faith in the Messiah, God renews the divine-human partnership with Israel. The nations have been grafted into the people of God in order to herald, embody, and participate in the mission of God. God's people, filled with the Spirit, are sent into the world for the sake of the whole creation in order to fill the earth with the glory of God through missional communities.

The church, empowered by the Spirit, participates in the ongoing ministry of Jesus. Believers embody Jesus's ministry in their own lives as disciples committed to following Jesus. The missional communities in the New Testament sometimes carried out their mission well (e.g., Acts 2–4), but other times performed poorly (e.g., Corinth).

The subsequent history of the church is an attempt to live out the story of God in Jesus. Living out the fourth act is a difficult task, much like it was for Israel. Sometimes the church has done this well, but other times poorly.

Yet God's eschatological purpose remains intact.

Act Five: Eschaton or New Creation

The Father will send the Son in the power of the Spirit to raise the dead, renew the creation, and unite God and creation in the new heaven and new earth (Rom. 8:19–23).

God's goal is the mutual indwelling of the Triune God with redeemed humanity as God dwells within a redeemed creation (the temple of God) where righteousness, justice, and peace fill the new creation (John 17:20–26; 2 Pet. 3:13; Rev. 22:1–5). This is the culmination of God's missional agenda.

This is the *restoration project* of God's grand narrative. God restores what is broken. But the goal is much larger. The eschatological goal is a renewal of the divine intent in creation itself, which is the union of God and humanity within the creation (Rev. 21:1–5).

This was God's intent from the beginning since the Father not only created *through* the Son in the power of the Spirit but also created *for* the Messiah (Col. 1:16). The Triune God always envisioned a future where God and humanity would unite in the person of the Son, share the divine rule of creation together, and dwell eternally in the new creation.

The Rule of Faith

This is God's missional story—(1) begun in *creation*, (2) restarted in *Israel*, (3) climaxed in *Jesus*, (4) continued in the *church*, and (5) fully realized in the *new heaven and new earth*. The story of salvation is an eschatological narrative.

This narrative is not only reflected in the biblical story but is summarized in what the early church called the "rule of faith." For example, versions of this common faith are found in Irenaeus of Lyons, Tertullian of Carthage, and Origen of Alexandria.[18] These rules of faith summarize the story that has shaped Christian reading of Scripture, teaching, worship, and life across the centuries (see Appendix One). This ancient rule of faith tells the story of creation, incarnation, and eschatological renewal, where the final goal is the union of God and humanity. This story lies at the center of Christian soteriology, and our ancestors in the Stone-Campbell movement embraced this grand narrative and lived as disciples of Jesus within it (see Appendix Two).

ESCHATOLOGY AND DISCIPLESHIP

Eschatology matters because God's goal defines the human vocation within the creation, contrasts with human brokenness, and entails the redemption of creation along with humanity. Eschatology provides the framework for thinking about the nature of salvation, and this fuels discipleship. God rescues the creation from its bondage in order that God might dwell within, enjoy, and share God's own eternal life with the creation.

When we recognize soteriology as a subset of eschatology, we see the larger dimensions of God's mission. It provides a way to grasp the personal, communal, and cosmic aspects of salvation, as well as its past, present, and future dimensions. Discipleship, then,

---

[18] Examples of the rule of faith are in Appendix One and in Everett Ferguson, *The Rule of Faith: A Guide* (Eugene, OR: Cascade Books, 2015), 1–15.

becomes more than "being good in order to go to heaven." Instead, it is about *participation* in the mission and life of God.

WHAT IS SALVATION?

Eschatology frames and gives meaning to the nature of salvation. That framing occurs through various intersections between the scope and timing of redemption in relation to God. The table below offers a visual summary of these intersections.

	Past	Present	Future
Personal	Forgiveness of sins and peace with God through Christ's faithfulness and the indwelling Spirit.	Living a Christ-like, transformed existence as new creatures in the Spirit.	Resurrection of the body animated by the Spirit as new creation.
Communal	The one body of Christ united to God in the Spirit.	The communal transformation of the church within history.	The full realization of the kingdom of God as community.
Cosmic	The inauguration of new creation by the resurrection and enthronement of Jesus.	The redemptive emergence of new creation in society and nature within history.	The full realization of new creation in the new heavens and new earth.

Rather than exploring each sector fully, we offer only a brief summary of elements vital to this discussion of discipleship.

Realizing the Past in the Present and Future

What God has already accomplished in the past is our present and future reality.

God's justifying verdict (forgiveness) found its rationale in the faithful obedience of Jesus the Messiah (Rom. 5:19). The past work of Christ secures our future. Consequently, we experience peace with God in Christ through the indwelling Spirit, even though our experience is sometimes plagued with doubt and despair. This salvation is personal, as we are saved as persons by persons (Father, Son, and Spirit) for relationship with persons (community). Thus, we have peace with God in the present because of what God has done in the past, and this peace is fully realized in the future.

God has already united all believers in the body of Christ through the outpouring and indwelling of the Spirit (1 Cor. 12:13). While the church does not appear united, it is "essentially, intentionally, and constitutionally" one.[19] God dwells in us, and we dwell in God. This mutual indwelling is God's goal, and the one for which Jesus prayed (John 17:21). We enjoy it even now, since God's poured-out Spirit has established that communal bond (John 14:23). We share the "communion of the Holy Spirit" (2 Cor. 13:14). Yet this is unrealized in the present. The visible church struggles to become what it is in God's eyes. Nevertheless, God has constituted the church as one in the Spirit, and God will fully realize this in the new heaven and new earth, even as we grieve over the present divided state of the visible body of Christ. As heirs of the Stone-Campbell movement, we yearn, seek, and work for the unity of the visible church.

God has already inaugurated the new creation through the resurrection of Jesus (1 Cor. 15:22). The resurrected Jesus is the new humanity—the firstborn of a renewed creation. The humanity of Jesus is not annihilated but transformed through an immortal body animated by the Holy Spirit (1 Cor. 15:45–46).

The resurrection of Jesus has injected a regenerating leaven into the cosmos, which will remake the cosmos in the image of the Son of God. The exaltation of Jesus assures us that death will be defeated, the creation will be redeemed, and humanity will be fully restored to its coregency with God in the cosmos. What God

---

[19] Thomas Campbell, *Declaration and Address* (Washington, PA: Brown & Sample, 1809), 16.

has already accomplished in the resurrection of Jesus by the Spirit, God will also bring to fullness for the whole creation in the new heaven and new earth.

Restoring the Future in the Present
What God will actualize in the future is already present in our experience.

God's strategy is to restore the future, a future already present in God's own life. The new creation is the future world imagined by Scripture, where the glory of God fills the whole earth. This kind of restoration does not reduplicate the past but seeks to realize the future in the present. We look to the past to see how that future has, at times, broken into human history and to learn from the Spirit-inspired witness of those who have imagined that future.

Personal sanctification is the process of becoming like Christ both inwardly and outwardly. Becoming like Christ involves moral transformation through the fruit-bearing power of the Spirit whom God has given us. We battle against the power of indwelling sin through the indwelling Spirit. It is a progressive struggle in which we are neither perfectionists nor moral defeatists. Victory comes through the cooperative grace of the enabling Spirit as we seek to follow Jesus.

The goal of this sanctification, both personal and communal, is what Eastern Orthodox believers call *theosis*—union with God. As participants in the divine community (John 17:21–23) and partakers of the divine nature (2 Pet. 1:4), we experience the depths of God's love in ways that are beyond mere cognition (Eph. 3:14–19). *Theosis* envisions not only our moral transformation into the likeness of Christ but opens our hearts to experience union with God through the Holy Spirit who cries "Abba" in our hearts (Gal. 4:4–6). Discipleship is empowered by this experience and shaped by our transformation into the likeness of Christ.

Present salvation is also the communal sanctification of the body of Christ. The church becomes the instrument of God's transforming work, through which the kingdom of God breaks into the world for healing, reconciliation, justice, and peace. Missional communities become alternatives to societal brokenness and thereby become both a witness to and a means by which the kingdom of God is present in the world. The church, filled with authentic disciples of Jesus, is *both a participation in the kingdom of God and a sign of the kingdom to come.* The church is both a promise and a presence of the future.

Because the church, sustained by the power of the Spirit, is a means toward the redemptive emergence of new creation, it embraces the task of social transformation as well as the care, enjoyment, and protection of the creation. Herein lies the importance of human vocation by which believers (and also, by God's grace, nonbelievers) participate in the mission of God to cultivate and redeem the creation. This is our identity as human beings. As junior partners with God, coregents in the creation, and cocreators of the future, God invests us with the dignity and joy of cooperating with God in the divine mission, which includes the emergence, growth, and development of creation's glorious future. *The task of discipleship is not only evangelism in the limited sense of inviting people to walk with Jesus, but it is also the renewal of the human vocation in our lives for which we were created in the beginning.*

Our careers are means by which we move the creation forward in redemptive, reconciling, and orderly ways. Believers should not choose their careers lightly, nor reduce them to moneymaking schemes. Believers become ministers in the kingdom of God as they use their careers to further the divine goal for creation and participate in the divine mission. Through this giftedness, expressed as love for neighbors and the creation, God redeems and renews the creation. We become instruments of the kingdom of God in the present as we anticipate the fullness of its future reality. Our careers, then, embody our identity as divine image bearers and enact our vocation as human beings.

Through these careers, we become instruments of the inbreaking kingdom. For instance, as environmental scientists, we protect and care for the creation. As medical personnel, we heal brokenness. As lawyers, we pursue justice. As economists, we work toward the elimination of poverty. As farmers, we feed the hungry. As debt collectors, we protect the debtor from abuse but seek justice for the creditor. As IT workers, we bring order to chaos and increase effectiveness. This is practicing the kingdom of God.

Nevertheless, creation will groan until finally liberated from death. While medical advancements cheat death, they do not defeat it. While justice grows, slavery still exists. While moments of reconciliation bear witness to new creation, much of humanity is still alienated from each other. The church, discipled by the ministry of Jesus and graced by God, bears witness to and works toward the goal. But only God's final act will fully reverse the consequences of human sin and make *everything* new.

Securing Boldness and Hope through the Future

What God will realize in the future grounds confidence and hope in the present.

Our glorification is our full transformation into the likeness of the new human, Jesus the Messiah. We pass from the old to the new in every way as the whole person, including the physical body, is rescued from death. Through union with Christ, recreated as divine imagers, we are united with God. This is *theosis*.

The hope of the Christian faith is not the *immortal soul* but the *immortal body*. Our salvation includes the redemption of our bodies (Rom. 8:23). At the same time, the inner person is perfected in God's love. While the process of perfection began in the past and continues in the present, it is not complete until we fully participate in the life of Christ at our resurrection. Then we, like Jesus, are permanently transfigured into the full likeness of God. This, too, is *theosis*.

Theosis is also communal as we fully participate in the dance of God's Triune fellowship. This is an eternal journey into the heart of God as we more deeply experience the love of the divine persons in their one fellowship. God will be new every morning, because as finite creatures, the infinite God will always have more to share. God is like a bottomless well from which we will eternally drink.

Just as we dance with God, we will also dance with each other. We will grow more intimate with each other. The relationships we have already begun will continue. More than that, they will grow deeper and wider, more intimate and more inclusive. The glorified community is not a static perfection but a dynamic growth into the heart of God and among the people of God. God will recreate a dynamic reality that invites the redeemed community to pursue growth, intimacy, and relationship within the new creation.

The kingdom of God includes the liberation of the cosmos from its bondage to decay (Rom. 8:19–23). Too often, Christians have thought they must escape the creation and fly away to an eternal heaven. We will, no doubt, escape the present evil age, but we will do so through God's renewal of the creation rather than its annihilation. The biblical story is not about escape but redemption. All creation will be called "holy" (Zech. 14:20–21), and the earth will know the righteousness, justice, and peace of the kingdom of God.

This is our hope, and it grounds our confidence so that we might live boldly in the world as the images of God and participate in the mission of God. This emboldens our discipleship in community, as we have a living hope and a certain goal.

CONCLUSION

The Christian faith is fundamentally eschatological, and our forebearers in the Stone-Campbell movement recognized this. Eschatology is about the future; but more importantly, it is about how everything relates to the future—how the whole story relates to the goal of the story.

The past assures the future. The work of Christ grounds our assurance. We know God is love because God has loved us in Christ. We know we are loved because the Word became flesh and dwelt among us. We know our future because God raised Jesus from the dead. We live neither in fear nor despair because we know what God has done in Jesus by the power of the Spirit. Despite the brokenness of the world, disciples know they are beloved by God and live in a beloved community.

The present yearns for the future. The gospel calls us to live in the world the future imagines. Believers live by the ethic of the new creation, rather than by the ethic of the present evil age. As believers live in the overlap of this age and the age to come, the Spirit calls us into and empowers us to live out the future in the present. This is the demand of discipleship. We follow Jesus in the power of the Spirit.

The future secures our hope. Broken and wounded, grief fills our world, and hopelessness often accompanies grief. The gospel announces hope, and it opens our eyes to the future. We lament injustice, violence, and death—and rightly so. At the same time, we herald victory because we know the future as well as the power of the Spirit in the present. Disciples not only proclaim good news; they embody that gospel in their words, actions, and dreams.

FURTHER READING

Bates, Matthew. *Salvation by Allegiance Alone: Rethinking Faith, Works, and the Gospel of Jesus the King.* Grand Rapids: Baker, 2017.

Gorman, Michael J. *Inhabiting the Cruciform God: Kenosis, Justification, and Theosis in Paul's Narrative Soteriology.* Grand Rapids: Eerdmans, 2009.

Hicks, John Mark, Bobby Valentine, and Mark Wilson. *Embracing Creation: God's Forgotten Mission.* Abilene, TX: Abilene Christian University Press, 2016.

Chapter Four

ENCOUNTERING THE LIVING WORD: SCRIPTURE

Now, while the philological principles and rules of interpretation enable many men to be skillful in biblical criticism, and in the interpretation of words and sentences; who neither perceive nor admire the things represented by those words; the sound eye contemplates the things themselves, and is ravished with the moral scenes which the Bible unfolds.

The moral soundness of vision consists in having the eyes of understanding fixed solely on God himself, his approbation and complacent affection for us. It is sometimes called a single eye, because it looks for one thing supremely.

—Alexander Campbell, *The Christian System* (1839)

The Bible must be interpreted. Churches of Christ have often denied this, assuming the Bible's function as Scripture is to provide truth or instruction directly and unambiguously. The inevitability of interpretation has pressed upon us historically nonetheless. Yet this chapter is about an opportunity. We believe that prioritizing our Trinitarian faith (Chapter Two) and the overarching narrative of Scripture (Chapter Three) when we interpret the Bible is the best way for Churches of Christ to move forward theologically. Our discipleship in community takes this practice, called theological interpretation of Scripture, as a way of encountering the living Word.

The early church also had to wrestle with Scripture's openness to interpretation alongside its faith in the Father, the Son, and the Holy Spirit. For example, from the second century to the fifth, divergent accounts of Jesus's humanity and divinity provoked heated debates (e.g., 1 John 4:1). The matter was progressively settled in the form of confessions known now as "ecumenical creeds."[1] Although Stone-Campbell leaders have often rejected the creeds as "the traditions of men," defensiveness about creeds can obscure the moral of the story. When we assume that the function of the creeds was to compete with or even replace the Bible, we fail to see what their actual function implies about the role of Scripture in the life of the early church.

Why did the ancient creeds develop? More to the point, why was there even disagreement among Christians about something as fundamental as Jesus's identity? Should not the teaching that gives meaning to our baptismal confession that "Jesus is the Son of God" be clear and straightforward? Should this not be the one point of doctrine that, without a doubt, can be settled by turning to Scripture? History forces us to answer these questions with honesty. Uncertainty, disagreement, and heresy did arise; Scripture alone did not provide certainty.

From this perspective, the creeds are an attempt to address how the church understands God and God's work as presented in Scripture. Specifically, the conclusions of the councils of the fourth and fifth centuries served to prevent the misinterpretation

---

[1] See Appendix One.

of Scripture on certain vital points, such as the identity of Jesus.[2] Thus, behind the hermeneutical function of the creeds lies the moral of the story: Scripture's meaning is not self-evident.[3]

This chapter reimagines the role of Scripture in the life of Churches of Christ for the twenty-first century. It begins by discussing some key features of our tradition's view of Scripture, with special attention to the trajectory set by Alexander Campbell. Next, a constructive vision of reading Scripture as the story of the Triune God is proposed. The chapter ends by offering some practical reflections on reading Scripture as disciples in community, in order to encounter the living Word today.

SCRIPTURE IN THE STONE-CAMPBELL MOVEMENT

There is much to affirm about the role of Scripture in the tradition of Churches of Christ, and the call for a shift of theological imagination is not purely about critique but also retrieval. Three dimensions of engagement with Scripture among Churches of Christ especially merit celebration: (1) the desire to be authentically a people of the Book, (2) the insistence that the pursuit of Christian unity not sideline Scripture, and (3) the practice of congregational interpretation. These three positive precedents are, in one sense, why Scripture must remain an inarguable keystone of the theology of Churches of Christ moving forward.

First, Churches of Christ have been proud to identify themselves as "people of the Book." This signals a core commitment: to let Scripture have the final say about Christian life. Rather than

---

[2] These issues were addressed in culturally particular terms and without reference to other vital matters that were not, at that time, contextually urgent. This observation does not, however, lessen the importance of the basic questions that *were* addressed.

[3] Hermeneutics is the field of inquiry that deals with the theory of the interpretation of texts.

treating Scripture as an object to be used, the church strains to hear God's voice in the text.

At its best, Stone-Campbell hermeneutics struggle to give Scripture the final word. The Command-Example-Inference (CEI) hermeneutic supposedly served to replace the subjective elements of perception and discernment with the objectivity of data. Whatever we might say about the failures of that struggle, it is necessary to affirm its aim. We are doggedly devoted to being a people for whom the book is really authoritative and formative. This commitment comes to expression in two areas: biblical preaching and biblical scholarship.

We have historically demonstrated a marked commitment to biblical preaching, and the textual sermon is the centerpiece of typical assemblies of Churches of Christ. The sermon is a mechanism for amplifying Scripture so that it rings loudest in our ears. It is the form of life through which Churches of Christ give Scripture the last word, week in and week out. We have also historically demonstrated a commitment to biblical scholarship.[4] Sadly, biblical scholarship often remains segregated from congregational life, ensconced in the academy (sometimes to church members' relief!). Still, biblical scholarship's importance in the tradition is indicative of our struggle to be authentic people of the book.

Second, our insistence on Scripture's role in Christian unity is characteristic of the tradition's engagement with Scripture. This amounts to a refusal to sideline the Bible, despite the difficulty of diversity in the pursuit of a shared confession of faith through worship, community, and mission. The Stone-Campbell movement's use of the motto "In essentials, unity; in opinions, liberty; in

---

[4] See Mark Hamilton, "Transition and Continuity: Biblical Scholarship in Today's Churches of Christ," *Stone-Campbell Journal* 9, no. 2 (Fall 2006): 187–204; James Thompson, "What Is Church of Christ Scholarship?" *Restoration Quarterly* 49, no. 1 (2007): 33–38.

all things, love"[5] bound essentials exclusively to Scripture. Before the addition of necessary inference to "express terms" (command) and "approved precedent" (example), Thomas Campbell stated in the *Declaration and Address* (one of the Stone-Campbell movement's earliest documents) that inferences should not be binding on Christian conscience.[6]

Thomas Campbell's approach to essentials assumed that inferences could be confined to the category of opinion, but the addition of supposedly "necessary" inferences to the developing hermeneutics of his successors indicates that the line between inferences and "the express authority of God" was not so easily drawn.[7] The early debate about whether human inference could play a role in forming theologically necessary conclusions was a step toward accepting the inevitability of interpretation. Unfortunately, even for those who affirmed necessary inference, that step did not challenge the assumption about Scripture's function in Christian unity. For the Stone-Campbell movement, Scripture continued to provide legal "terms of communion": a "perfect . . . constitution for the worship, discipline and government of the New Testament church" and a "perfect . . . rule for the particular duties of its members."[8] Yet the legal provision of "commands and ordinances" is not Scripture's only conceivable function in Christian unity. The rejection of a legal hermeneutic should not lead us to give up on Scripture playing a crucial role in the unity of the church.

---

[5] The motto has existed in various forms in various traditions before and since Stone-Campbell appropriation. See Hans Rollman, "In Essentials Unity: The Pre-History of a Restoration Movement Slogan," *Restoration Quarterly* 39 (1997): 129–39.

[6] Thomas Campbell, *Declaration and Address of the Christian Association of Washington* (Washington, PA: Brown & Sample, 1809); for the connection between this section and the motto, see Thomas Langford, "Motto of a Movement—A Reconsideration," *Restoration Review* 15, no. 10 (December 1973): http://www.leroygarrett.org/restorationreview/article.htm?rr15_10/rr15_10c.htm&15&10&1973.

[7] Campbell, *Declaration and Address*, 26.

[8] Campbell, *Declaration and Address*, 16.

The nineteenth-century Stone-Campbell movement intended to address the proliferation of denominations as Protestant interpretive freedom mixed with the antitraditional, individualistic spirit of newborn Americanism. By contrast, in the postmodern American stewpot of hypersubjectivity, cultural pluralism, and polarized public opinion, the challenges to unity are textlessness, apathy, and violent discourse. Therefore, the recontextualization of Scripture's role in Christian unity must involve (1) the rejection of radical relativism in favor of substantive essentials; (2) the advocacy of sincere discourse amid legitimate diversity of opinion; and, (3) in all things, the demonstration of Spirit-given virtues that make unity possible in the first place, such as love, peace, patience, kindness, gentleness, and self-control.

As we have stated in Chapter Two, the Trinitarian vision of God is an important starting point for contemporary Christian unity.[9] This is not enough by itself, however, because Scripture also has an important role to play. The tradition of Churches of Christ invites us to emphasize both the Trinity and Scripture in the pursuit of unity.

The final positive precedent for reimagining Scripture's role in the life of Churches of Christ is our tradition of congregational interpretation. Each local church accepts its own responsibility to God through the biblical text. This has often been called *congregational autonomy*. The definition of *autonomy* suggests what was historically at stake in congregational interpretation. Here, we encounter pivotal early American cultural mores: self-government,

---

[9] See also Christopher R. Seitz, ed., *Nicene Christianity: The Future for a New Ecumenism* (Grand Rapids: Brazos, 2001); Timothy George, ed., *God the Holy Trinity: Reflections on Christian Faith and Practice* (Grand Rapids: Baker Academic, 2006); and William J. Abraham, Jason E. Vickers, and Natalie B. Van Kirk, eds., *Canonical Theism: A Proposal for Theology and the Church* (Grand Rapids: Eerdmans, 2008).

freedom, and independence. Congregational autonomy enacted the rejection of institutional denominational authority—the *freedom* to establish congregational *self-government* on the basis of *independent* biblical interpretation.

The Stone-Campbell reaction to traditional, institutional authority is undoubtedly culturally conditioned and is arguably a culturally reflexive overreaction. Still, at best, it is freedom from the illegitimate exercise of human authority, not from the authority of God in Scripture. It is freedom to submit. The assumption of the local congregation's freedom to submit to the Bible over institutional determinations is still a positive precedent. For Churches of Christ, the noninstitutional disposition means that traditions are likewise subject to interpretation. This does not, however, amount to anti-institutionalism. The operative assumption is freedom to submit to Scripture when, upon returning once more to the text, we find new light that challenges traditional conclusions. This is far from a requirement to be against tradition, institutional stability, or contextually appropriate organizational forms of life. In fact, the anti-institutional disposition runs contrary to the freedom of the Stone-Campbell encounter with Scripture—freedom not to reject traditions that cohere with the text.

Congregational interpretation also presumes the whole congregation's participation in interpretation. We might call this the nonhierarchical disposition of Churches of Christ. True congregational interpretation takes the priesthood of all believers to its logical conclusion. This, in turn, forms the basis of a theology of church leadership that envisions the equipping of every disciple for participation in God's mission. Congregational interpretation also protects against the transfer of authoritarianism from the denominational level to the congregational level. Leadership at the local level is tasked to equip the saints for ministry. As shepherds and ministers guide the church in doctrinal and practical matters, open dialogue is a natural form of life for Churches of Christ committed to congregational interpretation.

The idea of church autonomy, if it is truly about submission to God, finally attests not to our freedom but to the radical freedom of God to work through Scripture, by the Spirit, in a local church, despite the limitations of its history, culture, and tradition. Likewise, the responsibility of the whole congregation points to God speaking to and through the whole people of God for God's purposes. In this way, Scripture plays the role of provocateur (one who provokes) and equipper. It disrupts the congregational status quo, provoking critical self-reflection and ongoing recontextualization, but also teaches and equips the church for mission (2 Tim. 3:16–17). Congregational interpretation, then, embraces the gift of freedom God offers through Scripture by challenging our assumptions and transforming our minds. We should not discard the expectation that the Spirit uses Scripture in this way.

These three positive precedents are each a different angle on the core of the Stone-Campbell movement: (1) the authority of Scripture (2) for the unity of the whole church (3) through congregational interpretation. Having affirmed the roles of authority, unifying center, and provocateur/equipper, we must consider how Scripture functions in them. To that end, we offer a brief critique of two key historical presuppositions of Churches of Christ regarding Scripture before proceeding to a theological proposal for today.

When it comes to the role of Scripture, two detrimental presuppositions have dominated the theological imagination of Churches of Christ: populism and perspicuity. In the context of early American Christianity, populism asserted the rights, wisdom, and virtues of the unequipped Bible reader. On the one hand, this is the "democratization" of American Christianity, in which the

Stone-Campbell movement profoundly participated;[10] this shift propelled the noninstitutional spirit of congregational interpretation. On the other hand, populism became anti-intellectualism.[11] The rights, wisdom, and virtues of the unequipped reader became antithetical to those of scholarly readers. Defensiveness and suspicion have become typical among "common" church people.

If populism is one side of the coin, perspicuity is the other. Whereas populism is about the capacity of the common person to understand Scripture, perspicuity is about the clarity of Scripture's communication. Unfortunately, in step with the anti-intellectual turn of populism, perspicuity transitioned from meaning "understandable" to meaning "self-evident." In other words, the claim of perspicuity has not always signaled that Scripture's significance is obvious and unmistakable, but it acquired this meaning in the early American religious climate.[12]

Advocating "the right of private interpretation," Robert Richardson represents the strong populist impulse of the early Stone-Campbell movement.[13] He believed the gospel, addressed to the poor and ignorant, was unequivocally "plain."[14] Richardson believed, however, that in regard to a variety of matters, the perspicuity of Scripture was relative to the reader:

> However brilliant the light of heaven, it may not penetrate eyes that are closed; however distinct and clear the truths

---

[10] Nathan O. Hatch, "The Christian Movement and the Demand for a Theology of the People," in *American Origins of Churches of Christ: Three Essays on Restoration History* (Abilene, TX: Abilene Christian University Press, 2000), 11–43.

[11] See Mark A. Noll, *The Scandal of the Evangelical Mind* (Grand Rapids, MI: Eerdmans, 1995), 63, 73–74, 95, 98.

[12] James P Callahan, "*Claritas Scripturae*: The Role of Perspicuity in Protestant Hermeneutics," *Journal of the Evangelical Theological Society* 39, no. 3 (September 1996): 367.

[13] Robert Richardson, "Interpretation of the Scriptures—No. II," *Millennial Harbinger* 3rd ser., 4, no. 8 (July 1847): 366.

[14] Alexander Campbell, "The Bible," *Millennial Harbinger* 3, no. 4 (August 1832), 341.

the Bible utters, they will fail to enter into ears that are dull of hearing; however interesting and attractive the objects it presents for acceptance, they can find no admission into hearts already full of grossness and corruption.[15]

Richardson did not prop up private interpretation on Scripture's inevitable clarity. He realized that the intellectual and spiritual capacities of readers affect the validity of their private judgments. Perspicuity stated as a confession of trust in Scripture's "power to impart knowledge" did not circumvent the subjectivity of the reader. Populism was not anti-intellectual, and perspicuity was not "a fixed law of interpretation," as it would later become.[16]

Campbell also admitted that some things in Scripture are hard to understand. Yet, he asked, "Is not the gospel one of the plainest things in all the divine communications, and are not all the christian institutions as plain as language can make them?"[17] The Stone-Campbell concern about the "institutions or ordinances" of the New Testament determined which parts of Scripture were "matters which are connected with salvation" and therefore necessarily plain.[18] Identified as essentials, these institutions obtain the privilege of being absolutely clear if the reader sets aside bias. This neutrality was not just a matter of being unprejudiced

---

[15] Robert Richardson, "Interpretation of the Scriptures—No. V," *Millennial Harbinger* 3rd ser., 5, no. 3 (March 1848): 137.

[16] Robert Richardson, "Interpretation of the Scriptures—No. IV," *Millennial Harbinger* 3rd ser., 4, no. 12 (December 1847): 702; Callahan ("*Claritas Scripturae*," 356) aptly calls this "perspicuity as hermeneutic."

[17] Campbell, "The Bible," 341.

[18] The phrase "institutions or ordinances" is taken from Alexander Campbell, *The Christian System*, 2nd ed. (Pittsburg, PA: Forrester & Campbell, 1839; repr. Nashville: Gospel Advocate, 1970), 314; cf. Robert Richardson, *The Principles and Objects of the Religious Reformation, Urged by A. Campbell and Others, Briefly Stated and Explained*, 2nd ed. (Bethany, VA: A. Campbell, 1853), 22: "the primitive institutions of Christianity, that is to say, of primitive modes of thought and action." These primitive modes of thought and action included especially, baptism, weekly communion, and church government.

by preconceived notions; the stubbornness of preconceptions reflected sinful pride—a spiritual matter.[19] In this sense, we might identify the setting aside of bias as repentance, which is a capacity of every reader. Unlike other matters, whose comprehension might require greater intellectual or spiritual capacities, these essentials were considered self-evident to a simple, fair-minded, repentant reading.

We are left with critical questions: how one decides what the essentials are and whether one can—or should—set aside the biases that Campbell presumed to take off like a pair of spectacles.[20] If Scripture's communicative power and intention does not actually function to present essentials self-evidently, then returning to moderate understandings of populism and perspicuity will open the way for Churches of Christ to reimagine Scripture's role today. Furthermore, combining these revised presuppositions with our other proposed theological commitments indicates a way forward. The next section will explore the possibility that the priority of Father, Son, and Spirit, along with the story of God in creation and redemption, provide the spectacles that we should intentionally put on, rather than attempting the "neutrality" of reading with no spectacles at all.

READING SCRIPTURE AND DISCIPLESHIP

As we reconsider the role of Scripture, it is best to recognize that Scripture functions as story. But making the Triune God our theological priority incites us to take the point further. Scripture functions specifically as God's story. It is a particular story with a plot that the ecumenical creeds specify. This is, to a great extent, what reading Scripture in light of the Trinitarian vision of God

---

[19] Campbell, "The Bible," 341; Richardson, "Interpretation of the Scriptures—No. V," 137.
[20] Campbell, "The Bible," 342–43.

means: letting the confession of the Great Tradition help us get the story straight.[21]

To engage Scripture as God's story is to listen to the narrative that tells of the Triune God's character, mission, and community. In this way, reimagining Scripture's role as God's story allows us to perceive its six essential functions in the life of the church.

The Nature of Father, Son, and Spirit: Character

Fundamentally, (1) *the church encounters God through the story.* This is a personal, relational encounter. Far from finding commands or moral tales, we find God. Quite apart from reading truth claims, we truly meet God through the story. Scripture's narrative permits the church to know God instead of merely knowing about God. Story does more than provide information; it occasions encounter.

The God we meet in the biblical story demonstrates many attributes. This character—which John sums up as love (1 John 4:8), Paul abbreviates as righteousness (Rom. 3:21), and Peter identifies as holiness (1 Pet. 1:15)—is multifaceted and awe-inspiring. The creative goodness, majestic power, faithful loving-kindness, and compassionate justice of the Lord become palpable, tangible, and shockingly intimate in the incarnate Word, full of grace and truth. The Father through the Son pours out the Spirit on the messianic people, and God's character becomes their character: "love, joy, peace, forbearance, kindness, goodness, faithfulness, gentleness and self-control" (Gal. 5:22–23).

---

[21] For a helpful discussion of the Great Tradition, see Roger E. Olson, *The Mosaic of Christian Belief: Twenty Centuries of Unity & Diversity*, 2nd ed. (Grand Rapids, MI: InterVarsity Press Academic, 2016), 29–49. For an introduction to the role of the creeds (the rule of faith) in "theological interpretation" of Scripture, see Joel B. Green, *Seized by Truth: Reading the Bible as Scripture* (Nashville: Abingdon, 2007), 79–85.

This final movement, in which the Spirit's virtues are manifest in the church, points toward the corollary of our encounter with God through the story: the restoration of God's image. As Scripture brings the community of disciples to encounter God, so it transforms us. We reaffirm the ancient expectation of Scripture's "usefulness" for "training in righteousness" (2 Tim. 3:16). Yet the key to understanding this function of Scripture is to realize that it hinges on the character of God. To be godly is to be like God; to be Christlike is to imitate Jesus; to be spiritual is to conform to the Spirit's nature. Too often, unfortunately, godliness is reduced to keeping commands, and Scripture's function is reduced to providing them. Instead, Scripture's usefulness has to do with the transformation of our character: "Godly life in Christ Jesus" (2 Tim. 3:12) contrasts with "having a form of godliness but denying its power" (2 Tim. 3:5). Our encounter with God in the biblical narrative produces "obedience," certainly, but this is the outworking of a transformed character: "since you have taken off your old self with its practices and have put on the new self, which is being renewed in knowledge in the image of its Creator" (Col. 3:9–10; cf. Gen. 1:26–27). Scripture's primary function in this regard is not to make moral demands but to tell the story that allows us to know God and therefore be "renewed in knowledge." In its narrative role, (2) *Scripture contributes powerfully to the restoration of God's image in God's people.*

The Purpose of Father, Son, and Spirit: Mission

If God is the protagonist of the story, God's mission is its plot. We will describe God's mission more thoroughly in Chapter Seven. At present, the concern is how Scripture functions in relation to mission. First, (3) *we are able to discern God's purpose through the story.* From a purely descriptive point of view, Scripture read as a story presents discernible narrative unity. It is a complex story, with many plot twists and a multiplicity of purposes at any given time, but the arc of the story also reveals a purpose singular enough to describe as the end (*telos*) toward which God the protagonist works. For now, we abbreviate this purpose in Peter's words: "to restore everything" (Acts 3:21). This is God's mission, the purpose for which the Father sends the Son, and they, in turn, send the Spirit.

Yet narrative does not invite us to description alone. The power of the story is its ability to draw us in, so that we perceive from the inside rather than describe from the outside. The story becomes our story, and so God's mission becomes our mission. This inhabitation of the story enables a different quality of discernment: we perceive God's purpose not only in reading the story but through living the story. It becomes the "spectacles" through which we discern God's ongoing work in the world as the story continues beyond the pages of Scripture. Only after the story becomes our way of seeing the world can we begin to recognize the new plot twists and particular purposes God is writing into the story today. Once the story's world becomes ours, our narrative sensibility increases, and recognition of continuity with the missional plot becomes critical for theological reflection.

Father, Son, and Spirit send the church to participate in God's mission specifically in this way: through the story. The Bible does not provide marching orders or instructions for mission. Those who struggle to live in step with the Spirit in a particular time and place know that those metaphors fall short when it comes to making decisions about new situations. What Scripture does as narrative is actually more powerful: (4) *its function is to draw us into God's mission and thereby give us an imagination.* Through a missional imagination, the church is able to practice theological discernment for its ongoing participation in God's mission.

The Relationship of Father, Son, and Spirit: Community

Finally, the biblical story functions—along with the sacraments of baptism and the Lord's Supper (see Chapter Six)—to create a community of disciples. This happens once again as two corollary movements. First, (5) *Scripture brings the church to share in the community of Father, Son, and Spirit through the story*. Jesus describes the disciples' inclusion in God's community: "... Father, just as you are in me and I am in you. May they also be in us... that they may be one as we are one—I in them and you in me—so that they may be brought to complete unity" (John 17:21–23). This undoubtedly pivots on the sending of the Spirit, the immersion of the messianic people in God's presence through baptism into the Messiah. Yet, although the Spirit moves where it will (John 3:8), we come to share in God's life by means of the apostolic testimony about the revelation of God through the Son (John 3:11–16; 17:20).

As John's tight interweaving of character, mission, and community hints, community is a result of sharing God's nature and purpose. Scripture transforms disciples' character and draws them into God's mission, creating a community of character and mission. Returning to Paul's notion of the renewal of God's image, we see its result is a community of reconciliation (Col. 3:11–17).

The corollary of inclusion in the community of Father, Son, and Spirit, then, is life as a community. Being clothed in God's image—compassion, kindness, humility, meekness, patience, and love—those reconciled to God from every nation and social class compose the community in which the message dwells. (6) *Scripture functions through the Spirit to create this community of reconciled reconcilers, of character and mission*.

READING SCRIPTURE IN THE LIFE OF THE CHURCH

Thus far, we have proposed six functions of Scripture's narrative role. Yet these functions do not seem to address the issue that has been front and center in the Stone-Campbell conception of Scripture: authority. Churches of Christ have, like much of Protestant Christianity, worked out their commitment to the authority of Scripture—a precedent we have reaffirmed—by engaging Scripture as a book of norms. By contrast, engaging Scripture as a normative story may leave us wondering how Scripture is authoritative.

How Narrative Norms

To explore this topic, we must begin again with God. The issue is not actually Scripture's authority but God's authority. As a community of disciples, we submit to God, not to the Bible. The question is, then, how does God exercise authority through Scripture? If Scripture's role is not that of a book of norms but that of a normative story, how then does narrative practically norm?

Certainty is the comfort we ultimately take from the book of norms. Yet there is no reason to think that God must exercise authority through our certainty, and Scripture may well be normative apart from providing certainty. Instead, the narrative establishes a normative trajectory, a way along which we travel together in the image and mission of God. When we live from within the story, we are subject to the authority of God. Scripture sets the direction, guides us, corrects our course. How we live along the way, however, is what theological reflection must determine: forms of life, ethical decisions, articulations of truth, and expressions of the message alike are subject to the discernment of the church in its context.

One powerful depiction of how narrative norms has been popularized by N. T. Wright. He likens the biblical narrative to a five-act play (see Chapter Three for a similar idea). It is as though church is a drama company, but part of the script has been lost. Wright notes:

The New Testament remains the standard by which the various improvisations of subsequent scenes are to be judged. That is what it means for the church to live under the authority of Scripture—or rather, as I have stressed all along, under God's authority mediated through scripture.

The New Testament offers us glimpses of where the story is to end: not with us "going to heaven," as in many hymns and prayers, but with new creation. Our task is to discover, through the Spirit and prayer, the appropriate ways of improvising the script between the foundation events and charter, on the one hand, and the complete coming of the Kingdom on the other.[22]

The metaphor of improvisation throws light on the nature of narrative normativity. Ours is not a scripted life. Yet the story is continuous, and our improvisation must cohere with the preceding acts as well as the end. The narrative arc is normative. Immersion into the story—familiarity from the inside—forms a sort of artistic sensibility, a theological imagination, which allows the church to act appropriately, faithfully, even though the situation is not scripted.

Eyes to See: Selecting Our Spectacles

Reading Scripture as story, as we have suggested, is how the narrative becomes the spectacles through which we see the world. The point is that we need to select our spectacles consciously and carefully. We may be tempted to place responsibility on the pulpit, but narrative preaching will not suffice. We are committed to congregational interpretation; therefore, we are bound to reform

---

[22] N. T. Wright, *Scripture and the Authority of God: How to Read the Bible Today* (New York: HarperCollins, 2011), 126–27.

congregational habits of reading. The whole church's imagination needs to discover anew the wide-open spaces of God's story. As Scripture's story forms the spectacles through which we read particular passages, in turn, these passages inform the whole, shaping our perception of the plot of God's story.

The biblical narrative is not, however, the only lens through which we should look at particular passages. We can also look through other sorts of lenses to see something otherwise imperceptible—like a telescope or a pair of 3D glasses. The ecumenical creeds, historical theology, and contemporary theology play a very significant role: through them, we perceive previously unseen dimensions of particular passages, which in turn can shape our vision of the whole story.

Likewise, we see from a particular theological point of view. Part of this book's proposal is that there are some theological "places" from which Churches of Christ engage in reflection. These places, in combination, provide a vantage point. It is not the only vantage point or the best—it is not a "God's eye view"—but it comprises places we can really explore, places that are ours to inhabit as a particular people. As we read Scripture, then, we should consciously and carefully establish our theological point of view. We hope the other chapters in this volume will provide guidance for purposefully placing ourselves as readers of the story.

Ears to Hear: Listening Carefully

In addition to seeing, Scripture offers another key metaphor for engaging God: listening. Eugene Peterson reminds us: "Listening is what we do when someone speaks to us; reading is what we do when someone writes to us. Speaking comes first. Writing is derivative from speaking. And if we are to get the full force of the word,

God's word, we need to recover its atmosphere of spokenness."[23] As Jesus put it, "Consider carefully how you listen" (Luke 8:18). Listening is relational. We know what a high compliment it is to say of a friend or spouse, "She's a good listener." Engaging Father, Son, and Spirit is not just about seeing; it is about hearing God speak to his people in Scripture. Relational reading is listening. Here are three practices for careful listening.

Spiritual disciplines. We need to reclaim the early Stone-Campbell commitment to charity in all things. As Churches of Christ have engaged Scripture, perhaps nothing has plagued us more than a lack of charity. We have too often managed to separate the intention to be godly from the way we listen to one another as fellow readers. If we are to escape our cycles of vicious divisiveness and move into fruitful dialogue about substantive issues, it is necessary to establish a commitment to spiritual formation for reading Scripture. That is, we must see the formation of character as rightly prior to congregational interpretation. Practically, we can assume a posture of charity toward one another by making spiritual disciplines the indispensable prerequisite for and accompaniment of biblical interpretation, not as an interpretive technique but as the means of becoming the kind of people who can listen to each other as God speaks to all. Hearing carefully entails charity in all things.

Missional praxis. Listening well also calls for practical involvement in mission before and during the interpretation of Scripture. Listening overlaps with doing—participating in God's mission. As participants in God's mission, we find ourselves in another place—a place in which we can hear more clearly. Like an ancient Greek amphitheater, mission provides an acoustic advantage. The

---

[23] Eugene H. Peterson, *Eat This Book: A Conversation in the Art of Spiritual Reading* (Grand Rapids, MI: Eerdmans, 2009), 87.

drama of God's story plays out with crisper sound as we read immersed in mission. Of course, it is no cure-all. Mission is not a procedure for taking control of the text once more. Rather, the essential claim is that the mission is God's, that God precedes us. Participation in God's mission is then a matter of going into places where God is already at work, encountering God's presence, discerning God's purpose, and bearing witness to it. When that happens, we inevitably return to the biblical text with a gift: recognition. The plot of the story resonates with our missional experiences. We hear the same voice in Scripture that we heard in the midst of mission. The story goes on, and playing a part in it engenders familiarity. Careful listening is participatory listening.

Communal discernment. Discerning the plot as it unfolds among us may not be easy—it certainly was not for the first-century church (the inclusion of the Gentiles being our primary case study in the New Testament). The storyline itself is what we might call perspicuous in the proper sense of the word; it is comprehensible though not self-evident. The story has plain meaning, but it may be rendered in a variety of expressions. Moreover, recalling our dramatic analogy, the plot continues between the first-century scene and the closing scene through discernment—faithful imagination and coherent improvisation. But as we gather around the text to encounter God the Father, the Son, and the Holy Spirit, the question of "How can I [understand] . . . unless someone explains it to me?" (Acts 8:31) becomes "How can I hear unless we read together?" Insisting that "I can" understand on my own does nothing to overcome these challenges in the twenty-first century. A final practical consideration, therefore, is how we discern the story's ongoing plot. For all that we might say hermeneutically, our first interpretive task in reimagining Scripture's role as story is to establish discernment as concretely communal. This implies a serious critique of our tradition's individualism: private interpretation may be a right, but in order to hear more clearly, we choose not to make use of our rights. Instead, as we gather around Scripture, we submit to one another, "For we were all baptized by one Spirit so as to form one body—whether Jews or Gentiles, slave or free—and we were all given the one Spirit to drink" (1 Cor. 12:13). Not all are given gifts of knowledge, wisdom, or teaching, but these are given to some for the equipping of the whole community for service (Eph. 4:11-12). The upshot is a need for congregational discernment processes conceived to include the whole community of disciples. On the one hand, programmatic inclusiveness ensures that we truly listen to one another without marginalizing some or ceding responsibility to a few. On the other, it permits those whom God has given for theological leadership to disciple the rest of the community in discernment and remain accountable to it. Naturally, congregational leaders shaped by Scripture and formed by God's Spirit must discern well for the spiritual good of the church. Nonetheless, congregations that listen carefully discern Scripture's implications in loving submission to one another. Theological interpretation of Scripture is, for Churches of Christ, a core commitment of discipleship in community.

FURTHER READING

Goheen, Michael W. *A Light to the Nations: The Missional Church and the Biblical Story*. Grand Rapids, MI: Baker Academic, 2011.

Green, Joel B. *Seized by Truth: Reading the Bible as Scripture*. Nashville: Abingdon, 2007.

McKnight, Scot. *The Blue Parakeet: Rethinking How You Read the Bible*, 2nd ed. Grand Rapids, MI: Zondervan, 2016.

Peterson, Eugene H. *Eat This Book: A Conversation in the Art of Spiritual Reading*. Grand Rapids, MI: Eerdmans, 2009.

Wright, N. T. *Scripture and the Authority of God: How to Read the Bible Today*. New York: HarperOne, 2013.

Chapter Five

PURSUING INTENTIONAL DISCIPLESHIP: THE BELIEVERS CHURCH

A proper literal Christian nation is not found in any country under the whole heavens. There is, indeed, one Christian nation, composed of all the Christian communities and individuals in the whole earth.

—Alexander Campbell, "Address on War" (1848)

Discipleship occurs in community, and this community includes the church—the community of fellow-disciples.

Church historians typically distinguish three views of the church that were prominent after the Protestant Reformation: Catholic (including Roman Catholic, Eastern Orthodox, and Anglican), Protestant, and Believers Church (or Free Church). The Catholic view conceives the church as an institution whose leaders are granted authority due to apostolic succession, an ancient pedigree that is traced back to the apostles and the churches they founded. In the Catholic view, salvation is mediated by the institutional church through the sacraments. In the sixteenth century, Protestants rejected the Catholic view in favor of another, more dynamic, vision of the church. For Protestant reformers like Martin Luther (1483–1546) and John Calvin (1509–64), the church exists by the Spirit wherever the gospel is preached, the sacraments are rightly performed, and salvation is appropriated by faith. The Protestants felt that this vision was more faithful to the gospel and avoided the corruption of the Roman Catholic Church at that time. Initially, both Catholic and Protestant views maintained a close connection between the church and the state. If one was born in a Catholic or Protestant state, then one was baptized, usually as an infant, and assumed the religion of one's state.

The Believers Church tradition is associated with the Anabaptists in Europe in the sixteenth century and some Separatist Puritans in England in the late sixteenth and seventeenth centuries. These believers were convinced that following Jesus is far more than being a good citizen of a Christian state. The church is separate from the state, and being a Christian includes a life of intentional discipleship. One becomes a Christian not by being born in a Christian state but by a confession of faith that is usually accompanied by believers baptism. Historically, in the Believers Church tradition, if one intentionally and unrepentantly lives in sin, then one may experience church discipline and be excluded from Christian community (based on Matt. 18:15–18).

Churches of Christ clearly stand in the Believers Church tradition. This is due partly to the fact that the Stone-Campbell movement emerged in the United States of America—a country where the Puritan experiment of the separation of church and state first took hold. There is no state church in the United States, although there is a cultural Christianity that is strong in large parts of the country. Churches of Christ, however, have traditionally viewed themselves as outsiders, sojourners, and those who take seriously the call to discipleship. Cultural Christianity is an ongoing temptation for Churches of Christ, but we hope that Churches of Christ will resist this temptation and continue to embrace the Believers Church vision, along with its emphasis on intentional discipleship.

Stone-Campbell leaders have devoted significant attention to ecclesiology, or the doctrine of the church. These leaders were committed to restoring the "ancient order," or the form of the church in the New Testament. But they also believed that the church itself is essential for ongoing growth in discipleship through worship, spiritual formation, and participation in God's mission. When the church gathers for worship, Christians commune together with God at the Lord's table, hear God's Word, and respond to God in songs, prayers, and the giving of financial gifts. Spiritual formation occurs in the assembly as disciples encourage each other and embody Christian virtues like love, humility, and generosity as examples for others to imitate (Heb. 10:24–25). In fact, early Stone-Campbell leaders viewed the worship assembly as one of three sacraments, along with baptism and the Lord's Supper. As a sacrament, the assembly is a means of divine grace through which Jesus's resurrection is celebrated and Christians are shaped into Christ's image by the Spirit's power.[1] We cover baptism and the Lord's Supper in more detail in the next chapter, but the sacramental view of the assembly in the Stone-Campbell movement is worth noting. Finally, the church is essential for discipleship in that God sends the church into the world to participate in God's mission of reconciliation. If Christians take discipleship seriously, then the church is not optional.

---

[1] For a fuller discussion of the assembly as a sacrament, see John Mark Hicks, Johnny Melton, and Bobby Valentine, *A Gathered People: Revisioning the Assembly as a Transformative Encounter* (Abilene, TX: Leafwood, 2007), 10–16.

THE BELIEVERS CHURCH AND THE STONE-CAMPBELL MOVEMENT

The Nicene Creed presents four classic marks of the church that are useful for exploring emphases of the Believers Church tradition in general and Churches of Christ in particular: the church is one, holy, universal (or catholic), and apostolic. These four marks, which are also rooted in the New Testament witness, describe the present identity of the church (what the church actually is in Jesus Christ, though the church often falls short of this identity), the task of the church (what the church is called to pursue with the Spirit's help), and the future of the church (what the church will be based on the promise of God). Although numerous leaders in the Stone-Campbell movement are representative of the Believers Church tradition, this chapter highlights Alexander Campbell (1788–1866) and David Lipscomb (1831–1917).

The Unity of the Church

The church is in fact one in Christ, but the Stone-Campbell movement emerged in a context of increasing division in European and American Christianity. The desire for Christian unity was central to the early Stone-Campbell restoration plea. Stone-Campbell leaders believed that by following the simple teachings and practices of the New Testament, the church would enjoy a real unity that also allowed for appropriate freedom of conscience. In Churches of Christ, this vision of unity includes a commitment to congregational autonomy, where local churches are led by a plurality of elders or shepherds (when qualified leaders are available; see 1 Tim. 3:1–7, Tit. 1:5–9). It is assumed that local churches will work together, and mainline Churches of Christ support parachurch organizations like schools, universities, children's homes, urban ministries, church planting organizations, and mission organizations. Participation in these organizations, however, is voluntary, and there are no formal church structures beyond the local congregation. The church maintains and experiences unity not through denominational structures but through its union with Christ, through a shared faith, and through shared practices like baptism and the Lord's Supper. All who are baptized in the Triune name are added to the church by God (Acts 2:41), and unity is the Spirit's gift (Eph. 4:3–5). In Churches of Christ, a spirit of unity among Christians is viewed as far more powerful than any imposed form of institutional unity.

David Lipscomb promoted the vision of unity and congregational autonomy that characterizes Churches of Christ. Lipscomb held a highly negative view of institutions in general, including human governments and all religious institutions beyond the local church that are "introduced under the pretext of bringing about greater unity and effectiveness than can be attained under what man regards as the looser and weaker provision made by God."[2] According to Lipscomb, God has already provided the church with everything necessary to accomplish the divine purpose, but many Christians, just like Israel in the Old Testament, reject God as king in favor of human kings (see 1 Sam. 8). Lipscomb believed that institutions beyond the local church were founded on sinful human desires, such as the desire to hurry along God's work or the desire to exercise power over others. These human institutions and innovations, however, are actually less effective than what God has already provided.

Lipscomb's opposition to the missionary societies of the northern Disciples, particularly the American Christian Missionary Society, illustrates his concern about human institutions. Lipscomb actively resisted these missionary societies because he believed they were a tool of northern Disciples to control and

---

[2] David Lipscomb, *Salvation from Sin*, ed. J. W. Shepherd (Nashville: Gospel Advocate, 1959), 294.

exert influence on southern churches. Lipscomb also felt missionary societies had a negative effect on mission work in that they encouraged local churches and individual Christians to feel less responsible for participating in God's mission. Furthermore, missionary societies allocated precious resources toward salaries for professionally trained administrators and missionaries. Lipscomb maintained that the southern churches were doing far more effective mission work than the missionary societies of the northern Disciples.[3] In some ways, Lipscomb's view is an extreme one for mainline Churches of Christ today, as many churches support professionally trained missionaries and parachurch organizations that promote mission work.[4] Still, Lipscomb's view illustrates well the ongoing emphasis on the local congregation for governance and ministry, and the voluntary nature of participating in parachurch organizations.

Lipscomb maintained that when Christians sincerely seek God and follow God's Word, then God's Spirit makes the church one. God's Spirit, not human institutions, secures Christian unity:

> We find that Christ and the Holy Spirit left the churches, the congregations, in different places, without any bond of union, save faith in God through a common Lord and Redeemer, and the bond of love that made each feel an interest in the weal or woe of all other human beings, and led all under the inspiration of divine love to work under the direction of the Spirit of God for the salvation of the world.[5]

---

[3] Robert E. Hooper, *Crying in the Wilderness: A Biography of David Lipscomb* (Nashville: David Lipscomb College, 1979), 162.

[4] A group of "noninstitutional" Churches of Christ continue to hold Lipscomb's view of parachurch organizations.

[5] Lipscomb, *Salvation from Sin*, 295.

For Lipscomb, what God has provided and what God desires is "a unity of spirit, a oneness of action growing out of the union with him, rather than a mechanical or organic union controlled by material force."[6] God's unity, grounded in the Spirit's work, helps Christians grow in the virtues necessary to maintain unity and serves as a check against the sinful desire to control others for selfish purposes. Further, only God's vision brings about an ideal "oneness with liberty."[7] God's plan allows individual Christians and local congregations to maintain a unity in Christ and the gospel while allowing the necessary freedom to follow personal convictions.

Unfortunately, Stone-Campbell heirs have experienced division from within, and Churches of Christ in particular have been tempted by a sectarian spirit. Lipscomb himself played a pivotal role in the formal division between the Christian Church (Disciples of Christ) and Churches of Christ when he agreed with the 1906 US Religious Census director that the two groups should be listed separately. Lipscomb continued to oppose certain practices of the Disciples, specifically missionary societies and instrumental music in worship; but for him, these practices were symptoms of larger differences between the two groups.[8] The division between these two branches of the Stone-Campbell movement brought Lipscomb deep personal pain and illustrates the difficulties and ongoing task of Christian unity. Nonetheless, if Christians are to pursue intentional discipleship today, then we must imitate Jesus by praying for and promoting authentic Christian unity (John 17:20–23).

---

[6] Lipscomb, *Salvation from Sin*, 296.
[7] Lipscomb, *Salvation from Sin*, 292.
[8] David Lipscomb, "The 'Church of Christ' and the 'Disciples of Christ,'" *Gospel Advocate* 49, no. 29 (July 18, 1907): 457.

The Holiness of the Church

The church is holy in Christ, but God also calls the church to pursue holiness with the Spirit's help. Synonyms for the word *holy* are *set apart* (2 Cor. 6:17) and, perhaps better because it is less likely to be misunderstood, *distinct*. The church cannot follow Jesus and be isolated from the world, but the church is distinct in that it engages the world as those who fully belong to God. The Believers Church tradition makes a clear distinction between the church and the larger society. The separation of church and state was a radical idea when first proposed by the Anabaptists in the sixteenth century and is one of the reasons why early Anabaptists faced intense persecution from both Catholics and Protestants. For many Anabaptists, faithful Christians cannot participate in the work of the state, especially in the areas of governing, policing, and warfare, since these require the use of violent coercion. These Anabaptists were strict pacifists who rejected all forms of coercion, especially violence.

Separatist Puritans adopted a similar vision of the church and state, but with one key difference: Puritans agreed with Anabaptists that the kingdom of God is the Christian's ultimate allegiance and is distinct from the kingdoms of the world. However, Puritans maintained that Christians may legitimately participate in the work of the state, including those areas that require the use of violent coercion. Both Anabaptist and Puritan visions of the Believers Church have been influential in the history of Churches of Christ. Early Stone-Campbell leaders like Barton W. Stone, David Lipscomb, and James A. Harding were pacifists and maintained an Anabaptist worldview.[9] At the same time, many early members of

---

[9] John Mark Hicks and Bobby Valentine, *Kingdom Come: Embracing the Spiritual Legacy of David Lipscomb and James A. Harding* (Abilene, TX: Leafwood, 2006), 146–49. Alexander Campbell was also opposed to war, but his pacifism sprang from a different source—his postmillennial optimism about humanity and history.

Churches of Christ came from Baptist and Presbyterian traditions, both of which emerged from Puritanism in England. Whether Anabaptist or Puritan in orientation, Churches of Christ have seen themselves as a distinct people in society who take Christian discipleship seriously.[10] Alexander Campbell defined the church as "[t]hat institution which separates from the world, and consociates the people of God into a peculiar community."[11] Lipscomb viewed the church as "essentially distinct and separate" from all earthly kingdoms.[12] The practice of believers baptism in Churches of Christ is grounded in the New Testament witness, but it is also related to the conviction that salvation is not a birthright of those born in a Christian state. Rather, salvation is God's gift that is appropriated by faith and accompanied by a life of intentional discipleship.

One way the church is distinct from society is in its moral holiness, or the moral convictions and virtues that Christians pursue. The Christian moral vision includes standards of personal conduct, but it is more than simply avoiding personal vices. The Christian life is one of following Jesus and embodying his life and teachings in our own lives and unique callings. The Christian life is also an ongoing transformation made possible by the Spirit's work, so that Christians grow to love and desire the things that God loves and desires. Because of the Spirit's work, Christians begin to put off "acts of the flesh" like "sexual immorality, impurity and debauchery; idolatry and witchcraft; hatred, discord, jealousy, fits of rage, selfish ambition, dissensions, factions and envy; drunkenness, orgies, and the like" and begin to display "the fruit of the

---

[10] This self-understanding is illustrated by the title of a late-twentieth-century history of the Churches of Christ. Robert E. Hooper, *A Distinct People: A History of Churches of Christ in the 20th Century* (West Monroe, LA: Howard, 1993).

[11] Alexander Campbell, *The Christian System*, 2nd ed. (Pittsburg, PA: Forrester & Campbell, 1839; repr. Nashville: Gospel Advocate, 1970), 55.

[12] David Lipscomb, *Civil Government* (Nashville: McQuiddy, 1913), 76.

Spirit," which is "love, joy, peace, forbearance, kindness, goodness, faithfulness, gentleness and self-control" (Gal. 5:19–23). Holiness is God's gift through Christ, but it is also a continual pursuit that is ultimately made possible because of the Spirit's work in us. Alexander Campbell stressed the profound transformation that accompanies new life in Christ:

> The Christian, or the new man, is then a philanthropist to the utmost meaning of that word. Truth and love have made him free from all the tyrannies of passion, from guilt and fear and shame; have filled him with courage, active and passive. Therefore, his enterprise, his capital enterprise, to which all others minister, is to take part with our Saviour in the salvation of the world....
>
> The character of the new man is an elevated character. Feeling himself a son and heir of God, he cultivates the temper, spirit, and behavior which correspond with so exalted a relation. He despises every thing mean, groveling, earthly, sensual, devilish. As the only begotten and well-beloved Son of God is to be the model of his future personal glory, so the character which Jesus sustained among men is the model of his daily imitation.[13]

For Campbell, the Christian is free from sin and fear, and thus free to love others and participate in God's mission in the world. The Christian has a new character and new desires that flow from a new status as an adopted heir in Jesus.

Similarly, David Lipscomb maintained, "What the church needs now is a consecrated membership that will sanctify the

---

[13] Campbell, *The Christian System*, 234–35.

man—soul, mind, and body, to the service of God."[14] For Lipscomb, holiness includes high standards of personal moral conduct, but it also includes active care for the vulnerable and hurting. Lipscomb demonstrated this active care most notably during the deadly cholera epidemic that struck Nashville in June 1873. Many who had financial means left Nashville during the deadly epidemic, but Lipscomb was among those who stayed behind. Lipscomb risked his own life to distribute food and supplies, care for the sick and dying, and transport Catholic nuns who also served the suffering via his buggy.[15] Lipscomb, in both his teachings and actions, sought to live a holy life of intentional discipleship.

The Universality of the Church

Universality, or catholicity, typically refers to the global nature of the church. Citizenship in God's kingdom is open to all through faith and baptism, irrespective of differences of race, ethnicity, socioeconomic status, and gender. Most certainly the Stone-Campbell movement, which is global in influence, participates in the universality of the church in this basic sense.[16] But the Stone-Campbell movement also promotes the universality of the church through an embrace of the theological principle of the priesthood of all believers. Early Stone-Campbell leaders affirmed that God calls the entire church to serve as God's royal priesthood in the world.

The Protestant reformer Martin Luther most famously articulated the principle of the priesthood of all believers. For Luther, this theological conviction extends in at least two overlapping directions. First, since all Christians are priests, then all Christians can do the work of the church, including praying for each other

---

[14] Lipscomb, *Civil Government*, 92.

[15] C. Leonard Allen, *Distant Voices: Discovering a Forgotten Past for a Changing Church* (Abilene, TX: Abilene Christian University Press, 1993), 92–109.

[16] See D. Newell Williams, Douglas A. Foster, and Paul M. Blowers, eds., *The Stone-Campbell Movement: A Global History* (St. Louis: Chalice, 2013).

and offering forgiveness in Jesus's name. Certain individuals may serve as public leaders and ministers in the church due to personal giftedness and God's calling, but these public ministers are only instrumentally different from the rest of the church. All Christians do the work of ministry, but for some Christians, this work of ministry includes public leadership in the church, preaching, and equipping others for service. Second, since all Christians are priests, then all legitimate vocations are holy and a part of God's work in the world. The full-time minister is not the only servant of God in the church. The farmer, teacher, entrepreneur, doctor, mechanic, and artist all participate in the mandate to cultivate God's creation (Gen. 1:28, 2:15) and minister to people through honest and beautiful work.[17]

Those in the Believers Church tradition embraced Luther's emphasis on the priesthood of all believers, and Puritans in particular broadened this conviction. Puritan ministers preached plain-style sermons, wore regular garments rather than priestly robes, and presided over simple and unadorned worship services. They sought to blur the distinction between the minister and the congregation, not in order to devalue the minister but in order to elevate the congregation and everyday life. The entire church is a royal priesthood, and all legitimate work is holy and of God.[18] Puritans, though, still maintained a distinction between the minister and the congregation through the authority of ordained ministers to administer sacraments. Only ordained ministers were to baptize and preside over the Lord's table.

---

[17] See John Dillenberger, ed., *Martin Luther: Selections from His Writings* (New York: Anchor, 1962), 64, 410.

[18] For a fuller description of the Puritans, see Justo L. Gonzalez, *The Story of Christianity*, vol. 2: *The Reformation to the Present Day*, rev. ed. (New York: Harper One, 2010), 194–95; and James F. White, *A Brief History of Christian Worship* (Nashville: Abingdon, 1993), 104–41.

The Stone-Campbell movement embraced and further expanded Puritan developments by rejecting the distinction between ministers and the congregation in the administration of the sacraments. Stone-Campbell churches were among the first to practice "lay presidency" at the communion table—a practice that continues in Churches of Christ today.[19] Churches of Christ practice weekly communion, and the one who presides at the table is typically not a minister but a member of the congregation. Further, in his 1843 debate with the Presbyterian Nathan L. Rice, Alexander Campbell denied the proposition that only a bishop or ordained presbyter should administer baptism. Campbell agreed that it might be appropriate for churches to typically ask recognized leaders to baptize, but nothing in the New Testament limits the authority of baptizing to ordained leaders. In fact, Campbell believed the early church spread so rapidly because all faithful and capable Christians were allowed to baptize and preside at the Lord's table.[20] The Stone-Campbell movement promotes a vision of universality that not only welcomes all people to membership in the church but also encourages the entire church to participate in God's mission in the world.

The Apostolicity of the Church

The Protestant reformers vigorously rejected the Catholic view of apostolicity. They argued that apostolicity is not a matter of churches and leaders having an ancient pedigree that is traced back to the apostles and the churches they founded, but rather is a matter of faithfulness to the apostles' teaching and way of life.

---

[19] White, *A Brief History of Christian Worship*, 168.
[20] Alexander Campbell and R. L. Rice, *A Debate on Christian Baptism* (Lexington: Skillman and Son, 1844), 567–610. For a summary of the debate, see Edward H. Sawyer, "Campbell-Rice Debate," in *The Encyclopedia of the Stone-Campbell Movement*, ed. Douglas A. Foster, Paul M. Blowers, Anthony L. Dunnavant, and D. Newell Williams (Grand Rapids, MI: Eerdmans, 2004): 145–47.

Stone-Campbell leaders embraced and expanded the view of the Protestant reformers through their commitment to the restoration plea and intentional discipleship. Churches of Christ seek to follow the simple teachings and practices of the New Testament churches, but the Stone-Campbell restoration plea is not simply about faithfulness to the past and restoring ancient practices. The restoration plea is also an attempt to restore the spirit of the early church—that is, the dynamism, unity, and freedom of the early church.

The desire to follow New Testament practices is seen in Churches of Christ in numerous places, including (1) the weekly celebration of the Lord's Supper and (2) the organizational structure of autonomous congregations led by a plurality of elders or shepherds. Another example is the commitment to congregational singing, traditionally a cappella singing. In fact, a cappella singing has become a distinguishing feature of worship in most Churches of Christ, although in recent years, the issue has become less divisive in progressive churches.[21] David Lipscomb, an influential proponent of a cappella singing, opposed instrumental music in congregational worship primarily because instrumental music is not explicitly authorized by the New Testament and is not found in early Christian worship. Here, Lipscomb's commitment to the "ancient order" and New Testament practices is clearly evident.

It is important to note, however, that Lipscomb combined his commitment to restoring the practices of the early church with his desire to restore the spirit of the early church. Living in an impoverished South that was decimated by the Civil War, Lipscomb

---

[21] For a good discussion of the instrumental music controversy in the Stone-Campbell Movement, see Everett Ferguson, "Instrumental Music," in *The Encyclopedia of the Stone-Campbell Movement*, ed. Douglas A. Foster, Paul M. Blowers, Anthony L. Dunnavant, and D. Newell Williams (Grand Rapids, MI: Eerdmans, 2004): 414–17. Ferguson offers a defense of a cappella singing in *The Church of Christ: A Biblical Ecclesiology for Today* (Grand Rapids, MI: Eerdmans, 1996), 268–73.

believed that musical instruments were a pretentious display of wealth that marginalized the poor. He also maintained that instrumental music in the assembly negatively affected congregational singing.[22] From Lipscomb's perspective, whenever churches would introduce instrumental music in worship, their congregational singing and participatory worship inevitably would decrease. Worship, for Lipscomb, was a participatory event that engaged the entire congregation. Lipscomb argued that a cappella singing was not only more faithful to the New Testament practice; it also encourages discipleship through participatory worship.

It is important to note that the Stone-Campbell restoration plea has several inherent limitations. First, contemporary biblical scholars rightly observe that the New Testament gives witness to some variety in the worship and organization of early churches.[23] This is clearly evident when one compares the worship assembly described in 1 Corinthians 14—the most detailed description of a worship assembly provided in the New Testament—to other New Testament examples and contemporary worship services. Second, from the beginning of the movement, the restoration plea has raised a number of questions regarding which beliefs and practices are included in the "ancient order." Such questions include: When should churches follow the strict example of the New Testament (even when there is no explicit command), and when is there freedom? When is freedom allowed in the different interpretations and applications of Scripture, and when is agreement needed for the sake of unity? These questions have been pressing, and divisive, throughout the history of the Stone-Campbell movement. And third, clearly some New Testament practices, such as washing feet and greeting with a kiss, are culturally conditioned and are

---

[22] Hooper, *Crying in the Wilderness*, 102, 159.
[23] Allan J. McNicol makes this same point in "Is the Stone-Campbell Movement an Identifiable Theological Tradition?" *Restoration Quarterly* 41, no. 2 (1999): 69.

not directly related to the apostolic testimony to God's work in Christ. Restoring such practices is unnecessary, encourages poor readings of Scripture, and moves the church's focus away from authentic discipleship.

Because of these limitations, we offer two proposals for understanding the Stone Campbell restoration plea. First, authentic apostolicity is not about restoring ancient forms for the sake of ancient forms. Rather, apostolicity is better conceived as following the teachings and practices of the apostolic testimony found in the New Testament. In other words, apostolicity is about following the teachings and practices that the apostolic church intended to pass on as part of its testimony to God's work in Christ. Second, this book began with an emphasis on God (the Trinity) and what God is doing in the redemption of creation (eschatology), because all Christian theology and practice is properly rooted in God and God's purposes. Starting with God and God's story clarifies the central beliefs and practices of the Christian faith and allows Christians to hold other beliefs and practices in proper perspective. In other words, not every issue is central to the identity and unity of the church. These two proposals do not settle every question, but they do clarify the central concerns of Churches of Christ and offer a better basis for prayerfully discerning contemporary issues. Apostolic churches are rooted in God and God's story, seek to follow the teachings and practices of the apostolic testimony, and pursue intentional discipleship.

THE BELIEVERS CHURCH AND THE EARLY CHURCH

The identity and purpose of the church are best understood in light of God and God's purposes. There are numerous images and analogies of the church in the New Testament, but three of the most prominent ones identify the church with the Trinity. The church is the people of God, the body of Christ, and the temple of the Holy Spirit.

"People of God" is first used in reference to the nation of Israel. God promised Abraham that through his descendants, all nations of the earth would be blessed. Because of God's promise, God brought Israel out of Egyptian slavery, entered into a covenant relationship with them, and settled them in the land of Canaan. Israel, the chosen people of God, was to be holy among the nations by worshiping God alone and seeking God's will above all else, including adopting a moral lifestyle that pursues righteousness and justice.

In the New Testament, the church is the continuation and fulfillment of Israel as Gentiles are grafted into Israel, the people of God. Just as Israel was to be a light to the nations, so the church, which is global in makeup, is to be a light to those who are far away from God.

> But you are a chosen people, a royal priesthood, a holy nation, God's special possession, that you may declare the praises of him who called you out of darkness into his wonderful light. Once you were not a people, but now you are the people of God; once you had not received mercy, but now you have received mercy.
>
> Dear friends, I urge you, as foreigners and exiles, to abstain from sinful desires, which wage war against your soul. Live such good lives among the pagans that, though they accuse you of doing wrong, they may see your good deeds and glorify God on the day he visits us. (1 Pet. 2:9–12)

For Peter, the church (which includes both Jews and Gentiles who put their faith in Jesus) is "a chosen people" and the true continuation of Israel. The entire church, not just a subset of leaders or a professional clergy, is a "royal priesthood," although the church has leaders who are tasked with shepherding the flock (1 Pet. 5:1–4). The church is "a holy nation" and "God's special possession" that lives among, but is distinct from, the rest of society. In fact, Peter calls Christians "foreigners and exiles" in the world. The church is holy, not in order to be isolated from the world, but in order to proclaim the praises of God in the world and to bring unbelievers to glorify God. Like Israel, the church worships God alone and longs for God's kingdom to extend throughout all nations.

"The body of Christ" is used in two ways in the New Testament. First, the church is compared to a human body that is made up of different parts with various functions. Each member of the church is valuable and needed for participation in the mission of God, just as every part of a body is important if it is to function properly (Rom. 12:4–8; 1 Cor. 12:12–31). Second, the church is called Christ's body, with an emphasis on union and solidarity with Christ (Eph. 1:22–23; Col. 1:18). As the body of Christ, the church participates in Jesus's ongoing ministry and is an extension of his presence in the world. Both uses of "the body of Christ" are important for understanding intentional discipleship, but the second one specifically relates to the identity and purpose of the church.

As the body of Christ, the church participates in the ongoing ministry of Jesus. Jesus's ministry, which Matthew and Mark summarize as the inbreaking of the kingdom of God (Matt. 4:17; Mark 1:15), is described in more detail in Luke's Gospel. In Luke, Jesus begins his ministry by reading from Isaiah 61 in a synagogue in Nazareth:

> "The Spirit of the Lord is on me,
>   because he has anointed me
>   to proclaim good news to the poor.
> He has sent me to proclaim freedom for the prisoners
>   and recovery of sight for the blind,

>to set the oppressed free,
>to proclaim the year of the Lord's favor." (Luke 4:18–19)

Jesus's reading from Isaiah is an expanded way of saying that in the words and actions of Jesus, the kingdom of God has come near. When God's reign is in our midst, the poor hear good news, the captive are set free, the blind are healed, and the oppressed receive freedom and mercy. Later, when John's disciples come to Jesus and ask if he is "the one who is to come" (Luke 7:20), Jesus's response echoes Luke 4:

> Jesus cured many who had diseases, sicknesses and evil spirits, and gave sight to many who were blind. So he replied to the messengers, "Go back and report to John what you have seen and heard: The blind receive sight, the lame walk, those who have leprosy are cleansed, the deaf hear, the dead are raised, and the good news is proclaimed to the poor. Blessed is anyone who does not stumble on account of me." (Luke 7:21–23)

Through faith and baptism, Christians experience a real union with Christ and become part of his body, the church. The church's role of participating in the ongoing ministry of Jesus is clear from the beginning of Acts, the second part of the two-volume work that includes the Gospel of Luke. Luke describes his Gospel as an account of "all that Jesus began to do and to teach until the day he was taken up to heaven" (Acts 1:1–2), with the assumption that Acts would continue to report the actions of the risen Lord through the church. In Acts, we see Peter, Paul, and the rest of the church teaching and doing the same type of things that Jesus taught and did. Just as Jesus proclaimed the inbreaking kingdom of God in his words and actions, so the church today participates in Jesus's ongoing ministry and anticipates the return of Christ, when all things will be made new.

"Temple of the Holy Spirit" is used to refer to the church as a whole (1 Cor. 3:16; 2 Cor. 6:16) and Christians individually (1 Cor. 6:19). The temple was the most important religious structure in Israel and the place where God was present among his people. In the New Testament, God's presence is no longer associated with a building but with a people, the church. The Holy Spirit secures the church's identity as one (Eph. 4:3–6), holy (1 Cor. 6:11), universal (Eph. 2:18), and apostolic (Eph. 2:19–22). At the same time, the Spirit empowers the church as it seeks to grow in unity (Eph. 4:3), holiness (Rom. 8:13; 2 Cor. 3:17–18), universality (Acts 1:8), and the truth of the gospel (John 14:15–17a; 16:7–15).

In the New Testament, discipleship is not an individual journey with Jesus but is one that includes and occurs within the Christian community. Throughout Acts, the church is portrayed as regularly meeting together for worship, mutual encouragement, and shared participation in God's mission (Acts 2:42–47; 4:32–35). During the first three centuries of the church's existence in the Roman Empire, the church was a persecuted minority that was distinct from the state. The Believers Church tradition maintains that the church is always an alternative community in the larger society. As Christianity appears to exert less influence in the West and beyond, the church will need to intentionally embrace its identity as an alternative community whose identity and purpose is rooted in God and God's purposes.

THE BELIEVERS CHURCH AND DISCIPLESHIP

A comfortable, cultural Christianity has always been a temptation for the church throughout its history. The Believers Church tradition takes seriously Jesus's call to discipleship and the identity and purpose of the church as the people of God, the body of Christ, and the temple of the Holy Spirit. Further, the Believers Church tradition elevates the local congregation as the primary, though not necessarily sole, locus of worship, spiritual formation, and participation in God's mission.

The Believers Church vision emphasizes the kingdom of God as the ultimate allegiance of Christians. All Christians have commitments that are an important part of their existence. Such commitments might include those to one's spouse, children, parents, local congregation, nation, political party, employer, schools, and social causes. These commitments are important but never ultimate. Christians have one ultimate allegiance: the Triune God. Jesus insists, "Anyone who loves their father or mother more than me is not worthy of me; anyone who loves their son or daughter more than me is not worthy of me" (Matt. 10:37). If we are disciples of Jesus, then he must be first in our lives. But it is only when we put God first that we can truly love—and, when necessary, oppose—our family, nation, local congregation, employers, and other commitments. The kingdom of God is the Christian's first priority and ultimate allegiance.

The Believers Church tradition envisions the church as an alternative community in society with a distinct ethical vision. The Believers Church tradition encourages Christians to embrace and become comfortable with their outsider status in society. As the Western world in particular becomes increasingly post-Christian, it is important for Christians to live and act as those who are "foreigners and exiles." The church will need to double-down on its efforts to pass along the faith—both its doctrinal teachings and moral beliefs—so that Christians can "give an answer to everyone who asks you to give the reason for the hope that you have" (1 Pet. 3:15). Christians should also be prepared to suffer in various ways for the faith.

It should be noted that an ongoing temptation for the Believers Church tradition is the tendency toward legalism and sectarianism. For instance, initially, the term *Puritan* was a derogatory one that was applied to Christians who sought a "pure" church where discipleship is actively pursued. Critics of the Puritans viewed them as morally strict, judgmental, and intolerant. Whether or not this caricature was always accurate, it does point to the real danger of legalism and sectarianism in the Believers Church tradition and one that, unfortunately, has characterized Churches of Christ as well. The church should care deeply about faithfulness to God and holy living, but the church follows a Lord who harshly condemned religious legalism and sectarianism. Balancing holiness, truth, and love is difficult, but God's Spirit is with the church and will help the church in its pursuit of intentional discipleship.

The Believers Church tradition embraces the task of growing in, and actively promoting, unity, holiness, universality, and apostolicity with the Spirit's help. The four classic marks are the present identity of the church based on Christ's work and the future of the church based on God's promise, but they are also tasks that the church is called to pursue with the Spirit's help. God calls the church to the ongoing task of growing in unity, holiness, universality, and apostolicity. Further, the missiologist Charles Van Engen notes that as a community of disciples, the church also functions as a unifying, sanctifying, reconciling, and proclaiming force in the world.[24] Faithfulness to the apostolic teaching must be combined with faithfulness to the apostolic task, which includes ongoing spiritual formation and proclaiming God's kingdom in the world.

The New Testament paints a beautiful picture of the church. The church's identity and purpose flow from the Trinitarian God, and the church is given other exalted titles such as the bride of

---

[24] Charles Van Engen, *God's Missionary People: Rethinking the Purpose of the Local Church* (Grand Rapids, MI: Baker Book House, 1991), 59–72.

Christ (Eph. 5:22–33; Rev. 21:2) and the children of God (Rom. 8:14–17). In a time when it is easy to denigrate the church, we should be careful to honor the church and be thankful for God's provision of Christian community. (1 Pet. 2:17). At the same time, we must remember that the church regularly falls short of its exalted identity and purpose. The church points people not to itself but to God. The church includes wheat and weeds, saints and sinners, growing together in the field, and even the finest wheat is still in the process of growth (Matt. 13:24–30). Still, discipleship takes place in community, and participation in the community of believers, the church, is crucial if we are to grow into the likeness of Christ.

FURTHER READING

Camp, Lee. *Mere Discipleship: Radical Christianity in a Rebellious World*, 2nd ed. Grand Rapids, MI: Brazos Press, 2008.

Ferguson, Everett. *The Church of Christ: A Biblical Ecclesiology for Today*. Grand Rapids, MI: Eerdmans, 1996.

Hicks, John Mark, and Bobby Valentine. *Kingdom Come: Embracing the Spiritual Legacy of David Lipscomb and James Harding*. Abilene, TX: Leafwood, 2006.

Love, Mark, Douglas A. Foster, and Randall J. Harris, *Seeking the Lasting City: The Church's Journey in the Story of God*. Abilene, TX: Abilene Christian University Press, 2005.

Chapter Six

EXPERIENCING GOD IN COMMUNITY: THE SACRAMENTS

All the ordinances of Christianity are means of grace. Faith, repentance, baptism, the Lord's day, the Lord's Supper, the church and its ministry are all means of grace.

—Alexander Campbell (1849)

Disciples walk a sacramental path stepped off by Jesus. From the waters of his baptism in Luke 3 to the table where he was made known as the resurrected Messiah in Luke 24, Jesus participated in the ordinances of Israel, invested new meaning in their rituals, and embodied the presence of the coming kingdom. Disciples follow Jesus from the baptismal waters to eucharistic tables, anointed with the Spirit and empowered for mission.

Sacramental theology accentuates a theocentric understanding of baptism and the Lord's Supper. God transforms believers through these appointed means in order to impart grace, assure the heart, and encounter believers in the power of the Spirit because of the work of Christ. We prefer the language of "sacrament" to "ordinance" because we want to emphasize what *God does* in baptism and the Lord's Supper rather than what *we do*. At the same time, we do not want to throw out ordinance language with the proverbial bathwater.

These gifts to the church are both an ordinance pledge (a commitment to discipleship) and a sacramental mystery (a work of God in believers). The mystery of the sacrament, however, is more fundamental than its pledging function. These gifts are effective *because* they are divine mysteries. The power of the sacrament is God's work, which we embrace through faith, and this sacramental work shapes and forms our discipleship.

Baptism and the Lord's Supper, as sacramental ordinances, are (1) *material* realities that (2) *represent* the truth of the gospel. These physical signs point to the work of God in Christ. They are also (3) *means of grace* that participate in the reality to which they point and are joined to it by the promise of God. They are (4) *eschatological* experiences because through them we participate in the present-yet-future kingdom of God. We are raised with Christ through baptism and eat with Jesus at the Messianic banquet. The efficacy of the sacraments, however, is not contained in the sign but is effected (5) *by the Spirit*, who mediates the grace of God, and we receive what God gives (6) *through faith*. The ground of God's gracious act through the sacraments is the (7) *reconciling work of Christ*.

The sacraments are a Spirit-generated experience of God's grace, as well as a human pledge of allegiance to the story of God in Jesus. They are divine pledges of faithfulness by which God communes with, assures, and transforms believers into the image of Christ through the Spirit. They are also moments in which disciples participate in the story of God, embrace their commitment to that story, and embody the reality of that story in their own lives.

SACRAMENTAL THEOLOGY IN THE STONE-CAMPBELL MOVEMENT

The Stone-Campbell movement historically practices three sacramental ordinances. "Here, then," Thomas Campbell wrote, "are the three grand comprehensive positive, ordinances of the gospel; namely, baptism, the Lord's Supper, and the Lord's Day," which are "designed to keep the blissful subject of our present and eternal salvation" before us.[1] Alexander Campbell called them the "positive institutions of the Christian system" and the "indispensable provisions of remedial mercy."[2] They are *"means of grace"* through which "the hand of God" writes upon our hearts the character of the Son.[3] In this chapter, we focus on baptism and the Lord's Supper, which is the primary marker of the Lord's day assembly. We regard the Lord's Supper and the Lord's day (assembly) as interlocking events, and the assembly was also discussed separately in the previous chapter.

Baptism

Although baptized as an infant in Scottish Presbyterianism, Alexander Campbell submitted to immersion in water as a believer in 1812 after restudying the question of infant baptism in the wake of his first child's birth. Campbell later defended believer's baptism in two debates with the Presbyterians John Walker (1820) and William L. McCalla (1823). In the latter, Campbell moved in a sacramental direction when he connected baptism with the joy and assurance of forgiveness. He thought some had reduced baptism "to the level of a moral example, or a moral precept." But Campbell

---

[1] Thomas Campbell, "An Address to All our Christian Brethren," *Millennial Harbinger* 3rd ser., 1, no. 5 (May 1844): 202.
[2] Alexander Campbell, *Christian Baptism with Its Antecedents and Consequents* (Bethany, VA: Campbell, 1851), 246–47.
[3] Alexander Campbell, "Regeneration," *Millennial Harbinger, Extra* 4, no. 5 (August 1833): 341.

invested baptism with soteriological significance as God's *"formal pledge"* of the believer's "personal acquittal or pardon."[4]

Following Walter Scott's successful revivalism in 1827, where Scott substituted baptism for the mourner's bench, Campbell wrote ten essays on the restoration of the "Ancient Gospel" in the *Christian Baptist*. There, Campbell described baptism not only as a *"sensible* [empirical] *pledge"* of forgiveness but also as a means of grace.[5] For example, he wrote, "forgiveness is through immersion,"[6] or baptism is a "medium through which the forgiveness of sins is imparted."[7] Baptism is not a "procuring" or "efficient cause," but it is an "instrumental cause."[8]

The fundamental impulse of Campbell's baptismal theology is assurance. He rejected the frontier search for assurance through a subjective conversion experience. Instead of calling the sinner to "pray through" at the mourner's bench, baptism itself is regarded as the sinner's prayer. It is both an objective moment of assurance and a means of grace.

All that is necessary for immersion is the confession that Jesus is the Messiah, with a commitment to follow Jesus. Every person "is a disciple in the fullest sense of the word, the moment" they believe and submit to this ordinance as a pledge to follow Jesus.[9] Baptism is an act of discipleship, and it is where believers commit themselves to the path of discipleship. Indeed, baptism

---

[4] Alexander Campbell and W. L. McCalla, *A Public Debate on Christian Baptism* (London: Simpkin and Marshall, 1842), 118.

[5] Alexander Campbell, "A Catalogue of Queries—Answered," *Christian Baptist* 6, no. 7 (February 2, 1829): 164.

[6] Alexander Campbell, "Ancient Gospel No. II," *Christian Baptist* 5, no. 8 (February 4, 1828): 166.

[7] Alexander Campbell, "Ancient Gospel No. VI," *Christian Baptist* 5, no. 11 (June 2, 1828): 254.

[8] Campbell, *Christian Baptism*, 256.

[9] Alexander Campbell, *The Christian System*, 2nd ed. (Pittsburg, PA: Forrester & Campbell, 1839; repr. Nashville: Gospel Advocate, 1970), 101.

is an "oath of allegiance" to the kingdom of God, according to David Lipscomb.[10]

Lord's Supper

"In the house of God," Campbell wrote, "there is always the table of the Lord."[11] Whenever the church gathers as the house of God on the Lord's day, the community sits at the Lord's table. As in Scottish Independency and most Christian communities, the celebration of the Lord's Supper is weekly. The Lord's day and the Lord's table are deeply connected.

Scottish and American Presbyterian tables, however, were often characterized by penitential spiritual disciplines, including meditation on Christ's sufferings, self-examination, and sorrow. Campbell complained the Supper had become "religious penance, accompanied by morose piety . . . expressed in . . . sad countenances on sundry days of humiliation, fasting and preparation."[12] That table summons "mourners to the house of sorrow," which is "as sad as a funeral parade."[13]

For Campbell, the table—a real gathering around a table every Lord's day—is saturated with festive joy. Christ "did not assemble them to weep, and wail, and starve with him," he wrote. "No, he commands them to rejoice always, and bids them eat and drink abundantly." We assemble to "eat and drink with him" at his table.[14] At the table, disciples are "honored with a seat at the King's table" and "eat in his presence."[15]

---

[10] David Lipscomb, "Unity of the Faith," *Gospel Advocate* 38, no. 20 (May 14, 1896): 308.
[11] Campbell, *The Christian System*, 267.
[12] Campbell, *The Christian System*, 175.
[13] Alexander Campbell, "A Restoration of the Ancient Order of Things.—No. VI: On the Breaking of Bread—No. I," *Christian Baptist* 3, no. 25 (August 1, 1825): 176.
[14] Campbell, "A Restoration of the Ancient Order of Things.—No. VI," 175.
[15] Campbell, *The Christian System*, 289.

Yet the dominant language of the early Stone-Campbell movement is commemorative, even "simply *commemorative*."[16] Without a vibrant sacramental theology where God does something at the table, Churches of Christ, for the most part, lost the festive joy envisioned by Campbell and reduced the table to its cognitive functions.

A. B. Lipscomb published a booklet on the Lord's Supper in 1917 (last printed in 1972).[17] The articles, consistent with twentieth-century Churches of Christ as a whole, primarily characterized the Supper as commemorative (memorial, monumental) and declarative (testimonial, proclamation). The former is more prominent than the latter, but both are cognitive categories. *We* remember, and *we* proclaim. Through this cognitive process, we contemplate the death of Christ, and when we do this together by eating and drinking, we proclaim the Lord's death. The table was effectively reduced to a mere ordinance.

At the same time, the table is a communal moment that binds believers together as disciples of Jesus. "Each disciple, in handing the symbols to his fellow disciple," wrote Campbell, "says, in effect, 'You are my brother. . . . You have owned my Lord as your Lord, my people as your people. . . . Let us, then, renew our strength, remember our King, and hold fast our boasted hope unshaken to the end.'"[18] The table, like baptism, is a weekly "oath of allegiance" to the kingdom of God as disciples of Jesus.[19]

---

[16] Thomas Munnell, *The Care for the Churches* (St. Louis: Christian Publishing, 1888), 251.

[17] A. B. Lipscomb, compiler, and John T. Hinds, ed., *Around the Lord's Table: A Series of Articles Written by Conscientious and Thoughtful Men about the World's Greatest Commemorative Institution*, 4th rev. ed. (Nashville: Gospel Advocate, 1950).

[18] Campbell, *The Christian System*, 273.

[19] David Lipscomb Jr., "The Lord's Supper," *Gospel Advocate* 58, no. 28 (July 13, 1916): 693.

Summary

In general, Churches of Christ embraced a sacramental understanding of baptism but an ordinance practice of the Supper. In other words, both are ordinances, but God only does something in baptism. Campbell envisioned more for the table, and he did not believe the ordinances were mere duties. While faith is the originating principle of obedience, love is its primary motivation. The ordinances themselves are "*means*" of "the enjoyment of the present salvation of God" in a community of disciples. Indeed, "all the wisdom, power, love, mercy, compassion, or *grace of God*, is in the ordinances."[20]

SACRAMENTAL THEOLOGY IN THE EARLY CHURCH

Sacramentality is much broader than baptism and the Lord's Supper. Sacramentality is the pervasive, active presence of God within the creation and throughout the history of God with humanity. Creation and history mediate God's presence and grace, and thus they express the inherent sacramental character of God's relationship with the world.

Baptism and the Lord's Supper, however, are concrete expressions not only of this sacramentality but also of the gospel of Jesus and the reality of new creation. They mediate the eschatological meaning of Christ's work.

The Biblical Narrative

God's story is a sacramental journey, analogous to the five-act drama of God's redemptive narrative outlined in Chapter Three.

Act One: Creation. Some reject sacramental mystery because it involves materiality and because they believe nothing external

---

[20] Campbell, *The Christian System*, 148–49.

or physical can mediate the spiritual. Ultimately, this rejection of sacramental mystery denies the goodness of creation. The creation is God's temple (Isa. 66:1–2). God rested in the creation and was present in Eden. Materiality does not hinder communion with God but mediates it. Every breath is communion with God. We experience this through nature walks, watching falling snow, or enjoying a beautiful sunset. We feel God's presence in such moments. In this sense, creation itself is sacramental.

Act Two: Israel. While some undervalue the rituals of Israel, they were sacramental occasions of God's presence. The temple was no mere symbol but the visible means by which Israel communed with God. Circumcision sealed God's promise, their sacrifices mediated forgiveness, their sacrificial meals were occasions of communion with God, and their assemblies "saw" God (Exod. 24:1–11). Though these ceremonies were brought to fullness in Christ, they were authentic experiences of divine presence within Israel.

Act Three: Messiah. The theological root of sacramental theology is the Messiah, who is the enfleshed sacrament of God. The incarnation sanctified creation—God became flesh. To polarize materiality and spirituality is to undermine the incarnation where the material and spiritual are united in the person of the Logos (Word). The gospel sacraments draw their meaning, power, and efficacy from this union in the incarnation. They are fundamentally Christological rather than ecclesiological since Jesus himself is sacrament. If flesh and deity are united in Jesus, God can unite materiality and grace in baptism and the Lord's Supper. Indeed, the latter is grounded in the former. Moreover, Jesus himself, as Incarnate God, participated in Israel's sacraments. He was baptized with Israel and ate at the tables of Israel's festivals. Jesus gave Israel's sacraments new meaning, depth, and significance. Jesus did not discontinue sacramental rituals. On the contrary, he kicked them up a notch. In the light of his resurrection, they became experiences of new creation mediated by the present creation (water, bread, and wine).

Act Four: Church. The church is the body of Christ, and God dwells in the body of Christ through the Spirit of God. We—finite, embodied people—are the habitation of God (Eph. 2:22). This is no figure of speech. We are sacramental beings; we live each moment as divine dwelling places. The church is flawed by its own sin, but it remains an authentic sacrament of God's presence.

Act Five: New Creation. The eschatological community of God will enjoy the full sanctification of the whole person in the new heaven and the new earth. We will live in a renewed heaven and earth in immortal, material bodies animated by the Holy Spirit, and God will fully rest in the new creation. "Holy to the Lord" will be inscribed on everything in that new creation.

Sacramentality saturates God's good creation, and the history of God's people with God is thoroughly sacramental. Baptism and the Lord's Supper, however, are God's gifts through which disciples of Jesus embrace the mission of God in the present creation and experience new creation. The sacraments, rooted in the reality of the incarnate Son and empowered by the Spirit, realize the future in the present. The sacraments mark our journey of faith from creation to new creation as disciples of Jesus.

Meaning of the Sacraments

In 1982, the Faith and Order Commission of the World Council of Churches adopted a significant ecumenical statement entitled "Baptism, Eucharist and Ministry" (known as BEM).[21] Widely distributed, it is frequently studied. BEM has become a consensus

---

[21] "Baptism, Eucharist and Ministry: The 'Lima Text,'" World Council of Churches, Faith and Order, paper no. 111 (World Council of Churches: Geneva, 1982), accessed May 29, 2018, http://www.oikoumene.org/en/resources/documents/wcc-commissions/faith-and-order-commission/i-unity-the-church-and-its-mission/baptism-eucharist-and-ministry-faith-and-order-paper-no-111-the-lima-text.

document in many ways, though differences remain and are noted in the document. For our purposes, the theology of BEM resonates with the best of sacramental theology among Churches of Christ.

BEM organizes the meaning of the sacraments around key theological ideas. As the product of a vibrant discussion of Scripture and the interaction of multiple Christian communions, the simplicity and depth of these points are captivating and summarize sacramental theology in a profound and helpful way.

Participation in Christ's life, death, and resurrection. The baptism of Jesus is our starting point (Luke 3:21–22). Our exodus through the water with Jesus is the beginning of a partnership with Jesus in ministry. Disciples follow Jesus into the water in order to follow him into his ministry. We pass through the waters not only to experience freedom from bondage but also to participate in the liberating ministry of Jesus.

Our baptism also participates in the death and resurrection of Jesus. We die with Jesus in baptism as our old person is crucified and a new one is raised to life. We transition from life to death. Dying with Christ, we die to sin and are thus freed from sin. Raised with Christ, we live again and are thus called to a life of holiness and righteousness (Rom. 6:1–7). We are freed not only from the guilt and power of sin but from the throes of death itself. This is the new creation that we presently experience in new life but also in the promise of resurrection.

Conversion, pardoning, and cleansing. Just as Jesus affirmed solidarity with sinners by submitting to a baptism of repentance for the forgiveness of sins (Luke 3:21–22), so we confess our sins in submitting to the same. The baptismal waters are a moment of repentance. They announce we have turned away from sin and pledged our allegiance to the kingdom of God. Through baptism, we commit ourselves to the ministry of Jesus as his disciples. More than mere human commitment, it is also a divine cleansing. We are washed, cleansed, justified, and pardoned (1 Cor. 6:11).

The gift of the Spirit. While the Spirit is active in the lives of people in many ways and diverse times, the gift of the Spirit is promised to the baptized (Acts 2:38). In fact, the key distinction between Jesus's baptism and John's baptism is the gift of the Spirit (Mark 1:4, 8; Acts 19:1-7), and Jesus is the one who baptizes in the Spirit. Like Jesus, God's presence is poured out on the baptized as a seal that they belong to God and are heirs of the new creation (Titus 3:5-7). This presence transforms us, empowers us, and assures our future in Christ. Baptism is an eschatological event where the Spirit anoints us just as Jesus was anointed at his baptism. Through the presence of the Spirit, we cry "Abba."

Incorporation into the body of Christ. When we are baptized into Christ, we are baptized into the body of Christ. We share a common baptism in which God unites us with Christ and anoints us with the Spirit. In the one Spirit, we are baptized into one body (1 Cor. 12:13). This union transcends all other allegiances and renders them radically secondary. There are no national, ethnic, gender, or social discriminations within the body, even as diversity is, at the same time, valued and honored. Our baptism means we are one, though diversely gifted. United in one communion in the Spirit, together we confess, serve, and praise the Triune God.

Sign of the kingdom. Just as John the Baptist prepared a people for the kingdom of God through a baptismal cleansing, so God translates us into the kingdom through a baptismal cleansing. We transition from the kingdom of Satan into the kingdom of God (Col. 1:13-14). Thus, through baptism, we are already members of the kingdom that has not yet fully arrived. Our baptism marks us as people who belong to the new creation and are committed, by the power of the Spirit and in the unity of God's people, to participating in that future reality now.

Thanksgiving to the Father. Jesus gave thanks to the Father at the table with his disciples (Luke 22:19–20). The Father supplies both the bread of creation *and* the living body of Christ that belongs to the new creation. We give thanks for bread as we recognize the gift of God's good creation, as well as how God became flesh for our salvation. As a meal, we are grateful for the nourishment God provides through the creation. But there is more. When we eat and drink, we give thanks for the Father's gift of the Son as we celebrate the work of God in Christ, since the bread, by the Spirit, is the body of Christ.

Memorial of Christ. Jesus did not tell his disciples to remember his death but to remember him (Luke 22:19). We remember what God has done for us in Christ and how Christ has acted on our behalf. We remember the incarnation, ministry, death, resurrection, and ascension of Jesus the Messiah. We remember the gospel. But this is no mere cognitive reflection on the past.Rather, it is the present experience of Christ. "To remember" is to experience the present reality of God in Christ reconciling the world to God. We "remember" our redemption every week, just as Israel "remembered" its own annually at Passover and weekly through its Sabbath assemblies (Lev. 23:3).

Invocation of the Spirit. Christ is present through the bread and wine by the work of the Holy Spirit. The Spirit is the one by whom we commune with the Father through the risen Christ. Just as Jesus was raised in the power of the Spirit, so we are raised to the heavenlies to feed on Christ, experience his living-giving presence, and commune with the Father through the Son in the Spirit (Eph. 2:18). The Spirit brings us to the Son and unites us with him in authentic communion, and we thus experience the "communion of the Spirit" in a concrete and embodied sacramental moment (2 Cor. 13:13). The eschatological Spirit transforms the old creation signs of bread and wine into the new creation experiences of the body and blood of Christ through which the living Christ nourishes us, assures us, and unites us.

Communion of the faithful. This meal nourishes the church and unites it through eating from one loaf and drinking one cup—that is, Christ himself. When we commune in the body and blood of Christ through eating and drinking, we bear witness to that unity, and we experience its spiritual and visible reality. This communion is not limited by space and time (Heb. 12:22–24). We are united with the church throughout the world and the people of God throughout time. We eat and drink as the one people of God despite our diverse geographic, ethnic, and temporal realities. The table, then, is an intensely communal event. We not only commune with the Father, Son, and Spirit, but we commune with each other as the Spirit unites the whole church—past, present, and future—in this eschatological moment of eating and drinking.

The meal of the kingdom. The future is already present at the table of the Lord as we sit at the Messianic banquet with all the people of God. The table in the church is the table of the kingdom of God that celebrates the reconciliation of all peoples, ethnicities, and nations, as well as the redemption of creation itself. The Lord's Supper is a foretaste as well as a present experience of the future. The Supper, then, calls us into the mission of God for the reconciliation of the world and the renewal of creation, and the Supper—which nourishes us with the power of new creation—transforms us into the image of Christ and empowers us for mission. We receive Christ to become Christ to the world—we eat the bread to become bread for the world, and we drink from the cup to pour out ourselves for the sake of others. The table sends us into the world. As disciples, we follow Jesus from the table to the cross.

PRACTICING WATER AND TABLE IN THE LIFE OF THE CHURCH

How does theology shape practice? Given the importance of these sacraments, do our practices cohere with their significance? Here, we propose some suggestions for our ecclesial community, that we might better align with God's will and Spirit.[22]

Baptism

Though many have a high view of baptism, some functionally reduce baptism to a private, brief, and isolated act of obedience. Others give more focused attention to a communal baptismal service (or liturgy). They wrap baptism in the clothing of Word, worship, and community, and they connect baptism with the grand story of the Christian Faith. We suggest six components for a more robust baptismal liturgy.

Tell the story. Let us join the Word with the water, because the gospel grounds, shapes, and gives meaning to baptism. Jesus is the Messiah, whose faithful obedience redeemed us from sin and death. The meaning of baptism, grounded in that story, can be told from several vistas—the flood, the exodus, the baptism of Jesus, the death and resurrection of Jesus, or Pentecost. Whatever the specific emphasis, baptism is a movement from the brokenness of this old creation to participation in God's new creation.

Rehearse our story. What we have in mind is something like what happens in Psalm 66. The Psalmist invites the community to first "come and see" as they remember together the story of how God delivered Israel from Egyptian bondage, refined them in the wilderness, and led them into a land of abundance. Then the Psalmist invites the community to "come and listen" to hear the

---

[22] Adapted from chapters 6 and 7 of John Mark Hicks, *Enter the Water, Come to the Table: Baptism and the Lord's Supper in the Bible's Story of New Creation* (Abilene, TX: Abilene Christian University Press, 2014), 119–44.

story of his or her own personal deliverance and invites them to join in his or her thanksgiving. In the same way, the first step in a baptismal liturgy is to proclaim the gospel, and the second step is for believers to rehearse their own faith journey. Everyone who walks to the edge of the water has a faith story. The community is encouraged when people share their stories.

Confess the story. Often, the baptismal confession is a simple "Yes." We do not undervalue that confession, but we suggest something more formative than a single word. Similar to the baptismal practice of the ancient church, we suggest something more like the Apostle's Creed or the Nicene Creed (the Latin *credo*, meaning "I believe"), which expresses the church's baptismal confession (see Appendix One).[23] It not only affirms the Triune story, but its rehearsal unites the believer with what the church has confessed throughout the centuries. The confession functions like a wedding vow—a statement of allegiance as well as trust. The confessor, for example, could repeat the words after the administrator speaks them. Acknowledging the work of the Triune God, candidates for baptism respond to the Father's act in Jesus through the Spirit by confessing the story and, through faith, vowing their commitment to live within it. In this way, we enter the story, own it through our baptism, and become disciples of Jesus.

Confess the Messiah. In one sense, including the good confession ("I believe that Jesus is the Messiah, the Son of the living God") is redundant, but we believe it is a poignant moment because it is central to the Gospel narratives themselves. In Matthew 16, Mark 8, and Luke 9, Peter's confession is a turning point. When Peter confesses Jesus as the Messiah, the Gospels turn to the

---

[23] Or something like Lipscomb University's "Statement of Faith," which tells the story of God. See "What We Believe," Lipscomb University website, approved by Lipscomb University's Board of Trustees on February 3, 2018, edited May 9, 2019, https://www.lipscomb.edu/about/christian-identity/what-we-believe/.

passion narrative. Immediately following Peter's confession, Jesus announces his coming cross and resurrection. When we make the "good confession," we announce our intent to follow Jesus by dying to self and commit ourselves to the path of discipleship.

Enact the story. Jesus went into the water praying, and we follow him into the water (Luke 3:21–22). Baptism is a prayer, and bathing it in prayer accentuates this point. Coming out of the water, Jesus hears the words, "You are my Son, whom I love; with you I am well pleased." We suggest speaking these words over those who rise from the water because the words belong to them as followers of Jesus. We might also acknowledge the descent of the Spirit, even symbolizing it through an anointing or a laying on of hands. Like Jesus, the baptized and anointed are empowered to endure the wilderness and practice the ministry of the kingdom as God's beloved children and disciples of Jesus.

In addition, our baptism participates in the death and resurrection of Jesus. This is a movement from sin to forgiveness, from slavery to freedom, from death to life. Through baptism, we are buried with Christ, raised with Christ, and seated with Christ. Baptism initiates us into new life. This is the experience of new creation itself, which entails participation in the communion of the Triune God ("baptizing them in the name of the Father and of the Son and of the Spirit," Matt 28:19), the communion of the saints ("baptized by one Spirit so as to form one body," 1 Cor. 12:13), and resurrection life ("we too may live a new life," Rom. 6:4). Baptism embodies new creation; it is a divine act of recreation.

Celebrate in community. Since Baptism is an exodus out of old creation (enslavement) into new creation (liberation), the model of Exodus 14–15 is instructive. The communal celebration of Exodus 15:1–2 should galvanize our own celebrations of baptism. Through baptism, we are plunged into a community that stretches across time from Israel into the future. We crossed the sea with

Israel, and now we rejoice with them. More than that, we join the heavenly chorus of praise among those who already stand by the sea with the Lamb, singing the "song of God's servant Moses and of the Lamb" (Rev. 15:3–4). Praise and song surround our exodus moments and this includes community.

We realize that baptism has become, for some, a private event. While this is sometimes appropriate—"that hour of the night" (Acts 16:33)—the communal meaning of baptism and its invitation for communal celebration locate baptism more solidly in the community itself. We hope baptisms might become more integrated into the assembly on the Lord's day and become part of the liturgical life of the church as it gathers weekly, even if only a video recording of the baptism is shown and the church gathers around the baptized on Sunday to celebrate.

Lord's Supper

We suggest six practices that might help a congregation more fully embody the theological vision of the Supper. We do not practice these every week ourselves. Sometimes they are present, sometimes not. This is a practical vision toward which congregations might move.

Practice One: Renew the meal. Every example of the Lord's Supper in the New Testament is a meal (Supper), and this reflects its antecedents in the Hebrew festivals, as well as the anticipated Messianic banquet in the new heaven and new earth. Nothing will invest the table of the Lord with "tableness" more than a meal—a meal in honor of, in the presence of, and in gratitude for Jesus. Meals renew the interactive communion of the table so that it is no longer silent and sorrowful but joyous and engaging. The Supper is not a funerary memorial but a thanksgiving meal celebrating our salvation. Meals, however, are more natural in small groups than large assemblies, which is reflected in the practice of the Jerusalem church in Acts 2:42–47.

Practice Two: Renew the table. We suggest people physically gather around a table at times, even if only for bread and wine. The literal table will produce the atmosphere of table—interaction and face-to-face communion. Stand around a table or sit at a table where Jesus is the host. At a minimum, a table is important for its symbolism. Even if we remain in our seats to eat and drink, a visible table symbolizes and embraces the spiritual reality of our faith.

Practice Three: Renew community. If we cannot gather around a table where community would occur naturally, we can renew the communal dimension in our eating and drinking through corporate prayers, corporate reading of Scripture, congregational singing, eating and drinking simultaneously, encouraging people to pray with each other, sharing the elements with those nearby, and encouraging each other through verbal interaction. Getting people out of their seats to commune, if even merely to stand or turn to people behind them to serve the bread and drink, can accomplish this in a small way. Invite people to come to the elements instead of bringing the elements to them. As people go to the elements, urge them to engage each other—hugging, greeting, and encouraging each other. The form in which many presently eat the Supper screams individualism and discourages active communion among participants.

Practice Four: Renew the mood. Restore the joy of the table as a thanksgiving. Most have been socialized into a silent, somber, and introspective meditation on the cross of Christ as the focus of the Supper. However, we do not commune with a dead Christ but a living one. Unfortunately, we often eat and drink like it is still Friday, the day of crucifixion, rather than Sunday, resurrection day. We set the mood by the prayers we pray, the words spoken, the songs sung, and the setting (seating arrangement, lighting, etc.).

When we recognize the living Christ at the table, we celebrate the joy of the table.

Practice Five: Renew the vision. A renewed theological vision of the table as a communal fellowship with the risen Christ is important for the process of embodying the fullness of the table. This vision embraces joy rather than memorialistic sorrow. We recommend prayer, teaching, discussion, communal processing, and more teaching, followed by more discussion and prayer. We also recommend varied practices that provide enriching experiences, including home meals and small group tables. Even if the above practices one through four are never implemented, a renewed vision and theological understanding will enable people to experience the Supper in more significant ways as they eat and drink within a visible community. Even in the most somber traditional service, we can still smile as we eat with the living Christ.

The presence of Christ does not depend upon an exact form—whether we sit at a table, walk down an aisle, or sit in a pew. It does not depend upon whether we sing before, during, or after the Supper. It does not depend on whether there is a meal or simple bread and wine. God effects the presence of Christ in the power of the Spirit when we eat and drink through faith. Form does matter when it subverts or hinders our experience of what God is doing. Nevertheless, as long as we do not undermine the gospel (as in the case of 1 Cor. 11), Christ is present.

Practice Six: Rehearse the story. We affirm the value and need for communion meditations. Communion meditations tell the central story of the gospel—that is, the one who became flesh for our sake, died for our sins, was raised for our justification, ascended to the right hand of God, is coming again to renew creation, and is even now the living host of this table. Communion meditations may tell the gospel story in creative ways, but there is no need for novel content. Believers confess this story, and it unites them around this table. At this communal table, we confess, commune with, and enjoy the living Christ.[24]

We affirm the weekly communion of the saints around the Lord's table. If the Lord's day celebrates the resurrection, then it makes sense to sit at the Lord's table with the risen Christ every first day of the week (Luke 24:1–8, 13–35; Acts 2:42–47; Acts 20:7–12), if not more often.

WHY THE SACRAMENTS MATTER

The sacraments are authentic experiences of God. They are not bare signs but divine acts. They are divine gifts through which we experience God, who comes to us in grace and mercy. They are, as Campbell said, "the gospel in water" and the "gospel in bread and wine."[25]

The sacraments serve our faith as moments of assurance and hope. God's word and promise are connected to these material signs. God assures us that Jesus is ours as surely as our bodies are washed in the water and our lips sip the wine. They are God's testimony that we are loved, and we testify to each other and the world that we are disciples of Jesus.

The sacraments are communal experiences of God. Baptism and the Lord's Supper are shared experiences through which God binds us together. We were baptized into one body, and we eat the one body of Christ together, united with the people of God in the heavenlies as well as throughout the whole earth. They are visible signs of unity, along with our shared commitment to follow Jesus.

The sacraments bind us to God's story in creation and redemption. We are united with Israel's exodus from bondage through the

---

[24] See Mark E. Powell, "Proclaiming the Gospel at the Table," *Christian Studies* 30 (2018): 95–104.
[25] Alexander Campbell, "Ancient Gospel. No. II. Immersion," *Christian Baptist* 5, no. 7 (February 4, 1828): 415.

water; their journey through the wilderness in their eating and drinking (1 Cor. 10:1–4); and their entrance into their inheritance, the Promised Land. We are united with Jesus as he is immersed in the Jordan, prays in the wilderness, feasts at the tables, dies on the cross, and ascends into the heavenlies in a resurrected body. We are united with the church throughout the centuries and into the future. We embrace the future of God's creation and experience the newness of redeemed creation as we share the resurrection of Jesus in our baptism and are nourished by the living Christ through the Supper. The story of God becomes our story through the sacraments, and through the sacraments we remember, embrace, experience, and commit ourselves to that story. And we bind ourselves to the story as an act of discipleship.

The sacraments empower mission and send us into the world for the sake of the world. Jesus was baptized in water, anointed with the Spirit, and commissioned to proclaim and practice the kingdom of God. In the same way, baptism commissions and sends us into the world to participate in the ministry of Jesus. At the table, Jesus serves and nourishes us so that we might become bread for the world. The table sends us into the world to sit at the tables where Jesus himself sat during his ministry. The water and the table form us as disciples of Jesus.

FURTHER READING

Hicks, John Mark. *Come to the Table: Revisioning the Lord's Supper.* Abilene, TX: Leafwood Publishers, 2003.

Hicks, John Mark. *Enter the Water, Come to the Table: Baptism and the Lord's Supper in the Bible's Story of New Creation.* Abilene, TX: Abilene Christian University Press, 2014.

Hicks, John Mark, and Greg Taylor. *Down in the River to Pray: Revisioning Baptism as God's Transforming Work*, rev. ed. Abilene, TX: Leafwood Publishers, 2012.

Stanglin, Keith, ed. *Christian Studies* 29 (2017). This issue is dedicated to studies on baptism. It is available here: http://austingrad.edu/Christian%20Studies/CS%2029/29%20(web).pdf.

Stanglin, Keith, ed. *Christian Studies* 30 (2018). This issue is dedicated to studies on the Lord's Supper. It is available here: http://austingrad.edu/Christian%20Studies/CS%2030/CS%2030.pdf.

Chapter Seven

PARTICIPATING IN GOD'S PURPOSES: MISSION

And, indeed, that which declares the philanthropy of God in the mission of his Son to be the Saviour of the world, that word of reconciliation which purifies the heart and reforms the life of man, is, the gospel, or word of God, contradistinguished from all other things written in the book. It is as much the object of these writings to reveal man to himself, to give a fair outline of the best and worst things in the history of man, and in God's government over man, as to reveal the character of God and his purposes concerning man.

—Alexander Campbell (1831)

Discipleship occurs in community, and this community includes the larger world into which the church is called to join in God's mission.

The gospel is fundamentally about God (Chapter Two) and the story of God's purposes for creation (Chapter Three). For many in Churches of Christ, however, the gospel has been reduced to the human response to the message, or what is traditionally called "the plan of salvation"—the five steps (hear, believe, repent, confess, and be baptized) that have characterized so many sermon invitations over the last century and a half. More recently, two concepts seem to dominate expressions of the gospel: the love of God and salvation from sin. The gospel, in this case, is not the news that a plan ensures personal salvation; it is the news that God's love ensures personal salvation. The shift from a mechanical proclamation to a relational one is significant, but ultimately it is the same essential news: salvation from guilt in order to "go to heaven" instead of hell. Both of these versions of the gospel are too limited and leave out the larger story of God's purposes, which Jesus summarizes as the inbreaking of God's kingdom (Mark 1:14–15). Jesus's proclamation of the kingdom immediately draws our eyes beyond our own personal destiny to the bigger picture of God's mission.

Jesus's message of the kingdom also situates briefer accounts of good news in a context that gives them meaning. So, for example, "For God so loved the world that he gave his one and only Son, that whoever believes in him shall not perish but have eternal life" (John 3:16) signals a much bigger story. Which God? The God of Abraham, Isaac, and Jacob—the Father of the Son. Which world? The world called into being by the "one God the Father all-powerful, Maker of heaven and of earth, and of all things both seen and unseen."[1] What Son? The incarnate Word, the Messiah of captive Israel. The specifics of this story are nonnegotiable for the biblical gospel.

Similarly, "that Christ died for our sins according to the Scriptures, that he was buried, that he was raised on the third day according to the Scriptures" (1 Cor. 15:3–4) can only function as a summary of the gospel if it is shorthand for the whole story that gives meaning to the title "Christ." "In accordance with the scriptures" is not a proof-texting ploy but is a reference to

---

[1] From the Nicene Creed in Jaroslav Pelikan and Valerie Hotchkiss, eds., *Creeds and Confessions of Faith in the Christian Tradition*, vol. 1 (New Haven: Yale University Press, 2003), 163. See Appendix One.

the whole of what Scripture claims. Death, burial, and resurrection only matter—are only good news for the world—if Jesus is Israel's promised Messiah, the descendant of Abraham and David. Thus, Paul writes a different summary to the Galatians and yet another one to Timothy: "Scripture foresaw that God would justify the Gentiles by faith, and announced the gospel in advance to Abraham: 'All nations will be blessed through you'" (Gal. 3:8); "Remember Jesus Christ, raised from the dead, descended from David. This is my gospel" (2 Tim. 2:8; cf. Rom. 1:3).

What is the gospel, then? In short, it is the whole story of God's purposes: creation and restoration, relationship and reconciliation, inauguration and consummation—and it is the story of humankind's place in those purposes. In other words, Scripture narrates the mission of God.[2] Humankind's rebellion results in God's offer of salvation being incorporated into the plot, and Scripture, written for our benefit, certainly highlights the problem of our sin in the context of this story. But even so, Scripture never loses sight of the larger story of God's purpose to redeem all of creation and draw God's people into the divine life.

Returning to the definition of the gospel, then, we come to an important conclusion: what God is ultimately doing in Jesus is about God's mission, and our "eternal life" makes sense only in reference to it. We are not merely saved from condemnation, as if that were the point of it all, but for a purpose—to participate in the divine life and mission. Two implications follow. First, God's purposes define the church's mission. The church's proclamation of reconciliation with God through faith in Jesus and the indwelling of the Spirit serves one of those purposes, but it is not God's only purpose. Second, the church is the assembly of participants: the

---

[2] For a masterful overview of the mission of God, see Christopher J. H. Wright, *The Mission of God: Unlocking the Bible's Grand Narrative* (Downers Grove, IL: InterVarsity Press Academic, 2006).

mission is not ours, nor are we its focus. Although mission work has often been thought of as church expansion, God's purposes extend beyond ourselves. The church plays a crucial role, having been gathered up into God's eternal plan (Eph. 1:3–2:10), but it is a role of servitude. Christians are blessed in order to be the means to God's good ends.

These two realizations—that God's purposes are primary and that the church is sent to participate in them—are at the heart of what has recently come to be known as the missional church movement.[3] The basic impulse of the missional church is to reorient theology toward God's mission in two senses. First, the missional church understands mission in terms of God's Triune life: the relationships of Father, Son, and Spirit, in which the church is included as a sent community. Second, the missional church understands mission in terms of God's purpose: the kingdom—of which the church is a "sign and foretaste" and an "agent and instrument."[4]

Missional theology is a proposal that, much like this book, begins with the end. The missional church looks toward the end of the story—the fullness of the kingdom—in order to discern the church's vocation in the present. The future kingdom interrupts the present as God works in the world. The missional congregation, seeking to collaborate in that work, conceives of its worship and life in the world as a response to the new thing that God is doing in its context. Rather than looking only backward to the first century, the missional church looks also to the present unfolding of God's mission and its future fulfillment. If the restoration of the first-century church is about restoring its nature and theology

---

[3] For the best overview of these developments, see Craig Van Gelder and Dwight J. Zscheile, *The Missional Church in Perspective: Mapping Trends and Shaping the Conversation* (Grand Rapids, MI: Baker Academic, 2011).

[4] Darrell L. Guder, ed., *Missional Church: A Vision for the Sending of the Church in North America* (Grand Rapids, MI: Eerdmans, 1998), 101.

as a sent community of kingdom ambassadors, then missional theology in the Stone-Campbell tradition focuses upon the belief that the church was always missional. The restoration of a more biblical church results in a more missional church. Many in Churches of Christ, however, would expect a chapter about "mission" to deal not with being sent but with being senders. Mission has been primarily about sponsoring cross-cultural mission work. Yet sending and being sent are two sides of the same coin. What has happened in recent history to catalyze the missional church movement—the shift from being senders only—is that God brought the insights of the cross-cultural missionary home to the sending church. Lesslie Newbigin (1909–98), an Anglican missionary to India, was especially influential in this regard. His theological work raised the critical question: What happens when we relate the gospel to our culture the same way cross-cultural missionaries relate it to other cultures? In other words, what happens when we realize we are all missionaries in missionary situations? Churches of Christ must return to Scripture in order to recapture the missional theology of the first-century church, but we should also pay attention to our history as senders, in order to bring home the lessons we have already learned.

MISSION IN THE STONE-CAMPBELL MOVEMENT

For both Campbell and Stone, the restoration of first-century Christianity would naturally lead to world evangelization: restoration first, then mission.[5] The logic of this progression was twofold. As a unifying initiative, restoration would banish the

---

[5] See, for example, Alexander Campbell, "Millennium—No. I," *Millennial Harbinger* 1, no. 2 (February 1830): 55; Barton W. Stone, "An Address to the Churches of Christ," *Christian Messenger* 6, no. 9 (September 1832): 266; Barton W. Stone, "On Missions to the Heathen Nations," *Christian Messenger* 13, no. 11 (March 1844): 330–33; Barton W. Stone, "The Editor's Remarks," *Christian Messenger* 9, no. 12 (December 1835): 280–81.

strife that undermined Christian testimony in the world. As a purifying initiative, restoration would advance the simple gospel instead of denominational dogmas, leading to the true conversion of the world to pure Christianity. The progression from restoration to mission helps us understand other dimensions of the missions history of Churches of Christ. The sequential priority of restoration morphed into a theological priority that led to restoration *over* mission and restoration *as* mission.

The Stone-Campbell movement's division over cooperative structures, most notably missions societies, is well-documented, and the emergence of Churches of Christ as a tradition was defined in part by the rejection of cooperation in missions.[6] By construing restoration in terms of congregational autonomy, mission became not only subsequent to restoration but secondary to it. Two qualifications are necessary. First, what became of mission in the tradition as a whole was not the intention of leaders like David Lipscomb, who argued against mission societies in large part because he thought relegating mission to the society would cause the church to lose its sense that "every Christian is a missionary."[7] Second, the point is not that restoration was contrary to mission work but that it was *over* mission. The priority of safeguarding the church against organizational structures "unknown

---

[6] See D. Newell Williams, Douglas A. Foster, and Paul M. Blowers, eds., *The Stone-Campbell Movement: A Global History* (St. Louis: Chalice Press, 2013), 30–45 and 76–93.

[7] David Lipscomb, "Concerning Armenia," *Gospel Advocate* 29, no. 2 (January 1887): 28. See also David Lipscomb, "Miscellany," *Gospel Advocate* 36, no. 44 (November 1894): 674. This was a pervasive idea in the late-nineteenth- and early-twentieth-century Stone-Campbell movement, in part due to the missionary society controversy, but also because it was a theological axiom that grounded opposition to missionary societies as opponents understood their function at the time. See, for example, J. G. Allen, "A Missionary Society That God Approves," *Gospel Advocate* 71, no. 3 (January 1929): 60; N. B. Hardeman, "The Church, and Its Mission," *Gospel Advocate* 47, no. 51 (December 1905): 803; A. B. Lipscomb, "A Plea for an Every-Member Church," *Gospel Advocate* 72, no. 32 (August 1930): 759.

to the New Testament" was ultimately detrimental to missions.[8] Churches of Christ have developed a vibrant tradition of missions despite our ambivalence about cooperation, but our practical ability to participate in God's work has suffered to the extent that restoration was a theological priority over God's mission.

The priority of restoration in Churches of Christ theology also carried the tradition into colonialist forms of missions. Colonialism in Christian missions is essentially the imposition of a culturally determined religious system, alongside political and economic systems, on a people group. Two interconnected tendencies often characterize colonialist missions: cultural proselytism (converting people to a culture) and church-centeredness (converting people to a church). Despite the assumption that the restored church was not culturally defined but purely biblical, these two tendencies combined in missions history of Churches of Christ in what we can call *restoration as mission*. The cultural arrogance common to most Western missions manifested among Churches of Christ in the expectation that only churches restored to the image of American restorationism could undertake legitimate world missions and that the form of American restorationism would be the product of missions.

The history of missiology in Churches of Christ is one of lagging behind wider trends and then rapidly closing the gap. In the mid-1930s, anthropology was emerging as a distinct field of study. It was not until the 1940s, however, that Eugene Nida, a Baptist linguist and Bible translator, "sparked the movement to

---

[8] See the "memorial" written to the 1892 General Christian Missionary Convention held in Nashville, Tennessee, reproduced in "All Delighted," *The Tennessean*, October 21, 1892, 8. For more information, see Doug Priest, "Missionary Societies, Controversy Over," in *The Encyclopedia of the Stone-Campbell Movement*, ed. Douglas A. Foster, Paul M. Blowers, Anthony L. Dunnavant, and D. Newell Williams (Grand Rapids, MI: Eerdmans, 2004), 534–36.

make anthropology a major component in missionary thinking."[9] His 1954 book *Customs and Cultures* was critical for mainlining anthropology into the church's missions consciousness. The next year, Donald McGavran, a former Disciples of Christ missionary to India, launched the church growth movement with his book *The Bridges of God*.[10] The church growth movement was also attuned to anthropological issues and became a major force in missiology.

Among Churches of Christ, the earliest effort to provide serious missionary training took place at Abilene Christian University from 1918 to 1924, but the professors involved left the school, primarily due to the evolution controversy of the 1920s.[11] In 1936, George Benson established missions courses at Harding University.[12] It was not until 1962 that George Gurganus began to teach the first graduate courses in missions at Harding School of Theology. He went on to establish a graduate program in missions at Abilene Christian University as well. Although Gurganus, a former missionary to Japan with a PhD in cross-cultural communication, did a tremendous amount to set Churches of Christ on a missiological path, the bulk of the missionary force remained disconnected from formal training. Nonetheless, from the 1960s onward, Churches of Christ missionaries were increasingly equipped with the latest in missiological theory.

---

[9] Charles H. Kraft, "Anthropology, Missiological Anthropology," in *Evangelical Dictionary of World Missions*, ed. A. Scott Moreau (Grand Rapids: Baker, 2000), 66–68.

[10] Eugene A. Nida, *Customs and Cultures: Anthropology for Christian Missions* (New York: Harper & Row, 1954); Donald McGavran, *The Bridges of God: A Study in the Strategy of Missions* (London: World Dominion Press, 1955; repr. Eugene, OR: Wipf & Stock, 2005).

[11] Chris Flanders, "The Beginning of Missionary Training in Churches of Christ," *Restoration Quarterly* 61, no. 1 (2019): 27–38; see also "The Beginning of Missionary Training in Churches of Christ (Part 2)," *Restoration Quarterly* 61, no. 2 (2019): 65–76.

[12] For a brief history of Churches of Christ missions training through the 1960s, see Alan Henderson, "A Historical Review of Missions and Missionary Training in the Churches of Christ," *Restoration Quarterly* 35, no. 4 (1993): 203–17.

Significantly, this shift occurred in tandem with the "rediscovery of grace in Churches of Christ."[13] A growing consciousness of both the gospel of grace, as distinguished from the legal reading of Scripture, and the cultural nature of the communication and embodiment of the gospel has created a tension between mission and restoration. As a result, some mission works of Churches of Christ in recent decades have set aside the emphasis on first-century church forms as they were identified in the late-nineteenth-century Churches of Christ in favor of culturally appropriate communication and embodiment—which is known generally as contextualization. To the extent that missionaries have found *restoration* to represent culturally American forms of church life, we might say that some have begun opting for *mission over restoration.*

There is a powerful tension here. The Churches of Christ remain deeply committed to the idea of the biblical church (see Chapter Four). Yet, by applying anthropological insights, missionaries have realized that different cultures determine what *biblical* means in different ways. Moreover, as missiology comes home to churches that have rediscovered grace but have not discovered a convincing alternative to the legal hermeneutic, the insights of missiology become increasingly important for theological reflection among American Churches of Christ.

MISSION AND THE EARLY CHURCH

God the Father, God the Son, and God the Holy Spirit are by nature missional. The basis of this claim is the sending (mission) of the Son and the Spirit. The substance of this claim is the purposefulness of God's relational nature: God has particular intentions as God relates to the world in love. The church's life "in Christ" is its

---

[13] Williams, Foster, and Blowers, *The Stone-Campbell Movement*, 226.

inclusion in the life of God and, therefore, in the purposefulness of God. Thus, the church is also missional by nature, insofar as it is a community of disciples restored to the image of Father, Son, and Spirit.

Yet the church may or may not participate as it should. This is as obvious as the decision to walk in step with the Spirit in regard to every other aspect of new life. What the observation about the missional nature of the church provides, though, is an understanding of what life in Christ is supposed to be: rather than just holiness, it is about holiness in purposeful relationship to the world. The image of God in which the church is re-formed and the life of God in which the church is included are that of the missional God. Participation in God's mission was the substance of the first-century church's life, and it is this life that Churches of Christ should seek to restore.

The Father's Direction: Reconciliation

What Peter describes as the restoration of all things (Acts 3:21), Paul envisions as the reconciliation of all things (Col. 1:15–20). God's purposes are cosmic, and Paul describes them as reconciliation. The Creator's relationship with creation is the essence of God's mission. In Christ is "new creation," and in him the reconciled become reconcilers, ambassadors of renewal (2 Cor. 5:17–21). So the church's vision of the end toward which God works—the work in which we participate—is the renewal of heaven and earth and the reconciliation of God with creation, which culminates in the declaration of the enthroned king: "I am making everything new!" (Rev. 21:5).

Missional theological reflection must account for both the scope and nature of these purposes. God is in relationship with all of creation as Creator, Sustainer, and Redeemer. What God is doing in the world before and beyond the church calls us to discern how and where God is working renewal and to collaborate according to God's image. Because Jesus is the image of the invisible God, we turn to the Son for greater understanding of God's way in the world.

The Son's Way: Incarnation
What prevents the church's mission from devolving into a colonizing force as it has before? Even the notion of being sent can become a way of objectifying those to whom we go. Concepts such as God's purposefulness and plan are vulnerable to cold, utilitarian construals. Then the church thinks of involvement in mission as a task to be executed strategically, making the people to whom we are sent into objects that must be evangelized, saved, or converted. At other times, the church acts as though participation means sole responsibility. Mission then begins to look like the attempt to govern on God's behalf and enforce God's will.

The first safeguard against such errors is the understanding of God's purposes that we have presented. Mission is relational to the core; reconciliation does not come through imposition but through acts of generosity, sacrifice, and kindness. And because mission is God's work before and beyond the church, by *sent,* the church does not understand itself to be taking God to the world. Rather, we find God already working reconciliation with others who are still enemies—just as we once were (Rom. 5:6–11)—and we bear witness in solidarity with them. In this, we find Jesus to be the model for the church's participation: he lays down his life for God's enemies to prove God's love for them.

Unless the Son took on flesh (John 1:14–18), he could not lay down his life. The incarnation was the essential first step—but not just so that he could experience death. The incarnation is the way that God's love became tangible and knowable (1 John 1:1–2). The Son entered completely into the life of humanity in order to relate to us on our own terms. It is in these terms that God's love is communicated by his death (1 John 3:16) but also by his friendship with those who need to know the Father's love (John 15:12–15). This friendship was evident in Jesus's ministry, particularly the stories of table fellowship. His opponents easily recognized his actions as "friendship" with tax collectors and sinners (Luke 7:34). As the one sent by the Father, Jesus related to those around him by giving and receiving hospitality and kindness. The cross, the ultimate expression of love, should be seen as the culmination of a lifestyle of reconciliation.

As the church follows Jesus into God's mission, cruciformity (cross-shaped-ness) is the mode of mission.[14] This means we understand our being sent in terms of the kind of life that Jesus exemplified in his relationships with the people for whom he died. Humility, self-denial, vulnerability, and suffering in solidarity with the world are the way the Son teaches the church to be sent.

The Spirit's Guidance: Transformation

The Father sets the direction and the Son teaches us how to walk, but the Spirit guides and empowers the church along the path of mission. In John's words, "But when he, the Spirit of truth, comes, he will guide you into all the truth" (John 16:13). We might misunderstand this guidance as merely cognitive, but that idea of truth is not John's. Truth is the first of all the revelation of God's glory in the person of Jesus, manifested inseparably as "grace and truth" (John 1:14, 17). The Triune God's revealed glory is his character, summarized by John as love:

---

[14] See Michael J. Gorman, *Becoming the Gospel: Paul, Participation, and Mission* (Grand Rapids, MI: Eerdmans, 2015); for discussion of the term *cruciform* in the context of Churches of Christ, see C. Leonard Allen, *The Cruciform Church: Becoming a Cross-Shaped People in a Secular World*, anniversary ed. (Abilene, TX: Abilene Christian University Press, 2016).

> This is how we know that we live in him and he in us: He has given us of his Spirit. And we have seen and testify that the Father has sent his Son to be the Savior of the world. If anyone acknowledges that Jesus is the Son of God, God lives in them and they in God. And so we know and rely on the love God has for us. God is love. Whoever lives in love lives in God, and God in them.
> (1 John 4:13–16)

The truth—that the Father sent the Son (John 17:8)—sanctifies the church as it is sent (John 17:17–18). The truth liberates Jesus's disciples from sin (John 8:31–32). The truth, ultimately, is Jesus himself: his way of life that leads to the Father (John 14:6). In other words, the truth is the Father's direction, in the Son, by the Spirit. The church is included in this way of true life and sent to love as God has loved, thereby *doing* the truth—liberating and sanctifying through love. As ever, this is the work of God; the church, as participant, is an instrument and a sign. Before the church, leading the church, is the Spirit, who convinces the world about Jesus (John 16:8). The church bears witness on the Son's behalf in symphony with the Spirit (John 15:26–27). This is the missional path along which the Spirit guides the church.

Paul similarly says, "Since we live by the Spirit, let us keep in step with the Spirit" (Gal. 5:25). We should resist the urge to reduce Paul's idea of being "led by the Spirit" (Gal. 5:18; Rom. 8:14) to a matter of individual spirituality—a state of piety we hope to achieve as an end in itself. A missional reading of these passages instead attunes our ears to the purposes of God at stake in Paul's argument. The transformation that the Spirit works in us—the "firstfruits of the Spirit"—are bound up with the hope of renewal for which creation itself longs (Rom. 8:23). The Father's cosmic purposes are never out of sight. As Paul argues for the law of love

(Gal. 5:14) and the fruit of the Spirit (Gal. 5:22-23), his conclusion is that "what counts is the new creation" (Gal. 6:15).

Paul's entire argument for the Gentiles' inclusion in God's people is an outworking of God's ancient plan to bless the nations. This purpose is the gospel as Paul understands it (Gal. 3:8; Rom. 15:8-9). The blessing of the nations through the chosen people of God (Gen. 12:1-3) has taken a couple of unexpected turns that require a long and difficult defense, to which Romans is dedicated. The first plot twist is the failure of the chosen people's sanctification through the law of Moses. The law intended to make Israel "a kingdom of priests and a holy nation" (Exod. 19:6). Their vocation as a priesthood for the rest of the nations was dependent upon their holiness, and Israel's unfaithfulness frustrated God's intentions to bless the nations. However, Paul argues that what the law could not do, the Spirit would. This is the essence of Romans 6-8.

The second plot twist is that the blessing of the Gentiles is actually their inclusion in the people of God—adoption into the family of Abraham (Gal. 3:7, 29; Rom. 4:11-12). As Abraham was blessed to be a blessing, so the Gentiles in Christ become the instruments of blessing for the rest of the nations. The power of the Spirit in the Roman Christians (Rom. 15:13) is the same power by which, according to Paul, Christ leads "Gentiles to obey God by what I have said and done" (Rom. 15:18-19). Reminiscent of John, Paul prays that "out of his glorious riches," Christ may strengthen the Ephesian Christians "with power through his Spirit in [their] inner being"—"power, together with all the Lord's holy people, to grasp how wide and long and high and deep is the love of Christ, and to know this love that surpasses knowledge—that you may be filled to the measure of all the fullness of God" (Eph. 3:16-19). Restated, the Spirit reveals the love of God, which is God's glory. The conclusion of this prayer is praise for "him who is able to do immeasurably more than all we ask or imagine, according to his power that is at work within us" (Eph. 3:20). Once again, it is a mistake to read these words in terms of what God will accomplish *for* us, though we often ask and imagine selfishly. It is rather a matter of what God's all-surpassing love will accomplish *through* us. "Through the church," the wisdom of the Creator is made known "according to his eternal purpose that he accomplished in Christ Jesus our Lord" (Eph. 3:9–11). Here also Paul is explaining the meaning of the Gentiles' inclusion in the people of God. According to his plan and purpose (Eph. 1:10–11), God has redeemed a people "created in Christ Jesus to do good works, which God prepared in advance for us to do" (Eph. 2:10). Harkening back to Israel's vocation as a royal priesthood and a holy nation, now the nations are being adopted, in the Spirit, into the household of God and formed spiritually into the holy temple where God dwells (Eph. 2:11–22).

John and Paul present a vision of the church's vocation in the power of the Spirit. The disciples of Jesus are liberated, sanctified, and sent according to God's ancient plan, to bear witness in word and deed to the reconciling love of God. Through the Spirit, in the Son, the church is transformed for the Father's mission.

DISCIPLESHIP AND MISSION

The church is a purposeful people—a community of mission. Perhaps this has always been an assumption, but the purposes the church served were not always God's. At times, the church has idolatrously determined its own ends. Far more often, we have simply diminished God's purposes to a fraction of our true vocation. God's people have always tended to develop theological nearsightedness. We fixate on our salvation and become self-centered. We concentrate on our holiness and become sectarian. We obsess about our worship and become neurotic. We focus on our expansion and become utilitarian. Salvation, holiness, worship, and growth are all among God's purposes, but they become distorted apart from the whole story of God's mission. Isaiah confronted Israel with a similar word from God. In the aftermath of judgment and destruction, the people of God would long for forgiveness, reconstruction, and peace. Those were promises God did in fact make through his prophets, including Isaiah. But then God put them in perspective:

> It is too small a thing for you to be my servant
>   to restore the tribes of Jacob
>   and bring back those of Israel I have kept.
> I will also make you a light for the Gentiles,
>   that my salvation may reach to the ends of the earth.
> (Isa. 49:6)

The restoration of Israel is simply too small a thing when the restoration of all things is at stake. The renewal of God's people serves a greater purpose. And we must not mistake the meaning of Israel's restoration. Isaiah's comparison is with a vision of God's people reestablished as they should have been: redeemed, worshipful, faithful, obedient, and holy. That is what God deems insufficient. That is what must be seen as a means to greater ends.

There is a first-century life to restore to the twenty-first-century church: its missional existence. Ours is the continuation of the same story that Isaiah told. As Jesus constituted his kingdom people, he took up Isaiah 49:6 and declared, "You are the light of the world" (Matt. 5:14). But the realization of our identity has proven as difficult for the church as it was for Israel. History has witnessed a church often unconvinced that it is too small a thing to have our sins forgiven and our brokenness mended. The restoration of biblical Christianity is, therefore, as urgent as ever. We must become once more a people who submit to the prophetic message of God's discontent with our mere existence as his people—for the New Testament church comprises all whom the Son sends by the Spirit to the glory of the Father.

The missional restoration of the church leads to a very different mode of theological reflection than simply restoring ancient forms. It invites us into the same kind of theological reflection practiced by the apostles and early church leaders. We must draw conclusions adequate for our twenty-first-century participation in God's mission as they did for their first-century participation. It compels us to approach theology as disciples called to participate together in God's mission.

SUGGESTIONS FOR ENGAGING IN THEOLOGY ALONG THE WAY

Mission is a location from which the church can engage in theology. The metaphor at work in this chapter is that of a journey. The Father's direction, the Son's way, and the Spirit's guidance compose the path of mission. As such, the journey is the location: the church reflects theologically along the way. The pilgrim people of God are in a process of theological discernment as God's mission unfolds among us. As the theology of participants in God's mission, missional theology seeks a vantage point from the inside. Experience has always been a part of Christian theology, and missional theology is an attempt to ensure that the church's experience is shaped by the encounter with God as participants in his mission.

Contextualization

Missional theological reflection happens in particular local contexts. As the message is embodied in distinctively local ways, congregations engage in the missiological practices of contextualization. We limit the discussion here to three practices for contextual theological reflection: self-emptying, questioning, and translating.

Self-Emptying

Modeled after Jesus's emptying of himself (Phil. 2:6–7), self-emptying is the church's initial commitment to let go of its own culturally conditioned traditions and preferences (even very positive ones) for the sake of identifying with its neighbors. Congregations convinced of the goodness and rightness of their current life must choose to embrace their being sent instead of "clinging to" an established way of life. The process of making this commitment as a congregation is not easy. Fear and traditionalism often motivate us, and the decision to begin self-emptying will require extended times of prayer and discussion. Moreover, the process is not quick. What Paul summarizes as "being found in appearance as a man" (Phil 2:7) includes Jesus's gestation, infancy, childhood, adolescence, and early adulthood. And why should the church expect transformation for mission to be quick and easy? "Quick" and "easy" signal the sort of cultural values at work in American churches of which we need to let go. What self-emptying attempts to accomplish is critical distance from culturally conditioned assumptions in order to bear witness to God's love in fresh ways. In short, self-emptying is the cultivation of theological humility.

Questioning

Once the initial commitment of self-emptying is made, the congregation can begin a process of intensive questioning. This process is directed at the congregation itself and at the surrounding culture. Questioning is not interrogation, however. It is a process of collecting stories. What are the stories the congregation tells itself about who it is and what it does week in and week out? What are the stories the culture recycles continually? These stories are contained in verbal story form but also in rituals, habits, and symbols. Stories are the primary way humans make meaning, and culture is, in one sense, the sum of that process in a given context. As congregations go through this process of questioning, they will discover that many of their culturally conditioned rituals, habits, and symbols (including church jargon) represent stories that their neighbors do not share. In light of questioning, it becomes easier to imagine how to retell the biblical story in culturally appropriate ways, not only verbally but also in terms of embodied communication. This process of retelling the biblical story in relation to the culture's own stories—whether by affirmation or challenge—is the third contextual practice, which we call translating.

Translating
Translating as a congregational process has to do with the way the gospel is restated in the practices of congregations. Many Churches of Christ stumble at just this spot, because our practices are presumed to be nothing more or less than biblical forms. Yet many forms, such as leadership and organizational structures, liturgy and music, and expressions of joy, fellowship, and reverence, require continual recontextualization. As congregations proceed from questioning to translating, they will begin to ask how to bring the biblical story into conversation not with their own stories but their neighbors'. The result will be an embodied rearticulation of the gospel—partly in order to communicate more clearly and partly because those neighbors will come to share the life of the church but continue to speak their language, like the crowd at Pentecost. At the same time, new sisters and brothers will assimilate the biblical story, even as the whole church reassimilates it continually in mission. Some of their stories will be transformed or discarded just as ours were, but the church's forms of life will inevitably come to reflect their story of redemption instead of just ours.

Participation

Missional theological reflection also happens in the places where God is at work, as the church's participation makes possible new experiential insight. Participation is about relationships of solidarity with the people—and the rest of creation—that God is redeeming. The church is sign, foretaste, agent, and instrument of the kingdom. Yet the church does not go into places of brokenness and poverty in order to represent the kingdom by simply being in those places. Rather, the church is able to represent the kingdom only by embodying reconciliation through authentic relationships.

Mutuality

Authentic relationships involve mutuality. Giving and receiving forms of generosity such as hospitality, openhandedness, and forgiveness are fundamental. Sharing grief and joy are also important modes of solidarity. Especially critical for theological reflection are listening and truth-telling. The missional church certainly seeks to embody and speak truth, but authentic relationship begins with listening and openness, and in this way, we are able to hear truth from our friends rather than presume it is our exclusive possession to share. Some of the greatest gifts in mission come to the church from people who are able to bear witness to God already at work among them. From such relationships, the church is able to reflect theologically in fresh ways. But the question remains: Relationships with whom?

The Margins

God, who wants all people to be saved, does not discriminate. Yet there is a clear socioeconomic inclination in Jesus's ministry. He chooses to spend a great deal of his time at the margins, among the outcasts, the sick, the disgraceful, and the poor. He does not reject the wealthy who seek him, and he is friends with and supported by people of means. Yet the kingdom of God that Jesus announces overthrows the injustice, poverty, disease, and violence that create the margins. The kingdom breaks in with a vengeance among the grieving, the downtrodden, the victims, and all those who do not participate in the abuses of conquerors and oppressors (Matt. 5:3–11). The kingdom is consonant with the Old Testament concern for the vulnerable of society, typified as the widow, the orphan, and the foreigner (Deut. 10:18; 27:19; Jer. 22:3; Ezek. 22:7; Zech. 7:10; Mal. 3:5). So central is this theme that James declares: "Religion that God our Father accepts as pure and faultless is this: to look after orphans and widows in their distress and to keep oneself from being polluted by the world." (James 1:27). Mission is not limited to but is inseparable from the margins. These are the places where the missional church's authentic relationships are most theologically generative.

God's mission is the place from which the church can explore theology as participants in God's purposes. Theology along the way is that of a trusting, hopeful, loving community of disciples that empties itself in order to live in solidarity with its neighbors. Such a purposeful people develops kingdom imagination, seeking to live as word-and-deed witnesses of reconciliation. Our struggle is to represent the kingdom through culturally sensible symbols. In mission, we continually develop forms of life that make sense of God's work in the world by retelling the biblical story in relation to our neighbors' stories rather than the church's alone. These forms of life are the substance of theology—the expressions of the missional church. Here is the invitation for twenty-first century Churches of Christ: to choose to live as a people sent toward the Father's direction, in the Son's way, by the Spirit's guidance. Along this path, there is a promise of theological renewal and authentic discipleship.

FURTHER READING

Allen, C. Leonard. *Poured Out: The Spirit of God Empowering the Mission of God*. Abilene, TX: Abilene Christian University Press, 2018.

Clark Moschella, Mary. *Ethnography as a Pastoral Practice: An Introduction*. Cleveland: Pilgrim, 2008.

Fitch, David E. *Faithful Presence: Seven Disciplines That Shape the Church for Mission*. Downers Grove, IL: InterVarsity Press Books, 2016.

Lau Branson, Mark. *Memories, Hopes, and Conversations: Appreciative Inquiry and Congregational Change*, 2 vols. Lanham, MD: Rowman and Littlefield, 2004/2016.

Roxburgh, Alan. *Joining God, Remaking Church, and Changing the World: The New Shape of the Church in Our Time*. Grand Rapids, MI: Baker, 2015.

Van Gelder, Craig. *The Ministry of the Missional Church: A Community Led by the Spirit*. Grand Rapids, MI: Baker Academic, 2007.

Wright, Christopher J. H. *The Mission of God's People: A Biblical Theology of the Church's Mission*. Grand Rapids, MI: Zondervan, 2010.

Chapter Eight

THEOLOGICAL COMMITMENTS IN CHURCHES OF CHRIST

As Jesus walked beside the Sea of Galilee, he saw Simon and his brother Andrew casting a net into the lake, for they were fishermen. "Come, follow me," Jesus said, "and I will send you out to fish for people." At once they left their nets and followed him.

—Mark 1:16–18

Then he called the crowd to him along with his disciples and said: "Whoever wants to be my disciple must deny themselves and take up their cross and follow me."

—Mark 8:34

The call of Jesus for us today is the same as for those who first heard him: "Follow me." Churches of Christ are a fellowship of Christian congregations devoted to intentional discipleship and to helping others follow Jesus.

Churches of Christ worship the one, sovereign God who is Father, Son, and Holy Spirit (the Trinity). The one God who is Father, Son, and Holy Spirit exists eternally in perfect community, and through Jesus and by the Spirit's work, humans are invited to share in the divine life and mission. By starting with the Trinity,

Christians emphasize the priority of God's action in our coming to know God, in our coming to salvation, and in our participating in God's purposes in the world. God cooperates with humans, and humans have some measure of free will to allow for authentic participation in the divine life and mission, but discipleship begins and ends with God.

Churches of Christ are committed to the story of God's work of creation and redemption as found in Scripture and affirmed in the rules of faith and ecumenical creeds of the early church. The Triune God created all things out of God's desire to share the divine life and purpose with human beings, each of whom bear the image of God. Yet, instead of embracing fellowship with God and participating in God's mission, humans created rival stories with evil and self-centered agendas. Because of human sin against God, now individual lives, communities, and all of creation exist in a state of brokenness and alienation. Yet God did not abandon his good creation but instead began to redeem it, first through Israel and ultimately through his Son, Jesus.

In Jesus, the eternal Son of God became fully human and truly embodied God's intent for creation. Anointed and empowered by the Spirit, Jesus proclaimed the inbreaking reign of God in his teaching and actions. Humans, as agents of the evil powers in the world, rejected and crucified Jesus, but God accepted Jesus's obedient death as a sacrifice to redeem humanity from sin and evil. God vindicated Jesus by raising him from the dead and exalting him to the Father's right hand, where Jesus lives and reigns today.

Through Jesus, God poured out the Holy Spirit on the church, the community of disciples. Anointed and empowered by the Spirit, the church participates in the ongoing ministry of Jesus in the world. Further, the church longs for the return of Christ, when God will raise the dead and judge evil, and God's people will enjoy eternal fellowship with him in a redeemed creation. It is this story, and this future hope, that has inspired Christian discipleship from the beginning of the church on Pentecost to the present day.

Churches of Christ are committed to hearing and following God's voice through Scripture, the Spirit-breathed Word of God. Through the reading and proclamation of Scripture and by the working of God's Spirit, humans encounter God, are transformed into God's image, and discern and participate in God's purposes in creation. Further, Christians are in a better position to encounter God through Scripture when they engage in practices like worship and spiritual disciplines, participation in God's mission, and communal discernment in a Spirit-filled church.

Churches of Christ are committed to the unity, holiness, universality, and apostolicity of the church, the community of fellow-disciples. The church includes all Christians who have confessed faith in Christ, been baptized, and pursue a life of discipleship. Further, the church community is essential for growth in discipleship through worship, spiritual formation, and participation in God's mission.

The church is one. Churches of Christ affirm the autonomy of the local congregation under Spirit-led leaders. Participation in religious organizations beyond the local church is encouraged but voluntary. The church maintains and experiences unity not through denominational structures but through its union with Christ, through a shared faith, and through shared practices like baptism and the Lord's Supper. Unity is the Spirit's gift, and the Spirit desires for all Christians to grow in a spirit of unity and love.

The church is holy. In Christ, the church is God's holy people who are called to be holy in the world. Christians follow Jesus by embodying his life and teachings in their own lives and unique callings. With the Spirit's help, Christians pursue moral principles and virtues grounded in Scripture and the Christian faith. The Christian life is one of ongoing transformation made possible by the Spirit's work so that Christians grow to love and desire the things that God loves and desires.

The church is universal. God's kingdom is the ultimate allegiance of Christians. Citizenship in God's kingdom is open to all through faith and baptism, irrespective of race, ethnicity, socioeconomic status, and gender. God calls all Christians, as God's royal priesthood, to cultivate creation through their vocations and to participate in God's work of redemption.

The church is apostolic. Churches of Christ seek to follow the simple teachings and practices of the apostolic testimony found in the New Testament. With the Spirit's help, Churches of Christ also seek to embody the spirit and way of life of the early church. The church is apostolic to the extent that it proclaims and embodies the apostolic witness to Christ, is led and empowered by God's Spirit, and participates in God's mission.

Churches of Christ are committed to sacramental practices like baptism and the Lord's Supper, through which God communicates grace and humans pledge themselves to discipleship. Through faith and by the Spirit's power, the church encounters God and is spiritually transformed through simple, material practices like baptism and the Lord's Supper. In baptism, believers participate in Christ's life, death, and resurrection; receive forgiveness of sins and the indwelling of the Spirit; and become part of the church, the body of Christ. In the Lord's Supper, the church enjoys table fellowship with God through the risen and present Lord, remembers and gives thanks for what God has done in Christ, and anticipates the feast to come in the new creation. Like the early church, Churches of Christ celebrate the Lord's Supper every Sunday.

Churches of Christ are committed to participation in God's mission. The Father is at work reconciling all things through Christ and bringing about new creation. Led and empowered by the Spirit, the church participates in Jesus's ongoing work in the world. Just as Jesus emptied himself in the incarnation and crucifixion, so the church follows Jesus's path of love and humility to proclaim the gospel to all people—especially those at the margins of society. Churches of Christ pursue the missional restoration of the church, which includes proclaiming the gospel and demonstrating God's love to all people, listening ever anew to Scripture, discerning together the Spirit's guidance, and seeking to be faithful to God's purposes today just as the early church was in the past.

RESPONSE

Lauren Smelser White

In *Discipleship in Community*, the reader finds that Powell, Hicks, and McKinzie have put together an extensive selection of theological goods, each worthy of close and ongoing attention. The assortment is so far-reaching and attention-worthy, in fact, that it is hard to settle on a starting place in responding to the project as a whole. Perhaps it is easiest to begin by saying what I find most promising about it—its situating the Stone-Campbell tradition in fruitful relation with the so-called Great Tradition of Christian thought. Rather than consigning the former to its sectarian impulses, or endeavoring simply to translate classical orthodoxy to Restorationists, Powell, Hicks, and McKinzie establish an *interchange* between the Stone-Campbell heritage and wider Christian orthodoxy, thereby enhancing the doctrinal focal points under consideration. Happily, then, though this book will most naturally draw notice from readers with vested interest in the Churches of Christ, it could be very useful to persons of any background. This is, to my mind, the best sort of "ecumenical strategy": the sort wherein thinkers appreciatively engage adjoining belief systems without apologizing for their own particularity (i.e., for their denominational inheritance and formation) but, rather, exhibit readiness both to critique that heritage and to celebrate the assets illumined there when set in conversation with neighboring thought.

On following Powell, Hicks, and McKinzie's various "ecumenical excursions" in these chapters, I was happy not only to be reminded of features of the Stone-Campbell tradition worth retaining (particularly when augmented by insights drawn from classic Christian thought), but also to discover some of those features for the first time. Among those new to me were Alexander Campbell's Trinitarian commitments, examined in Chapter Two. The authors make no bones about the modernist "hesitancy toward the Trinity and religious mystery" that undergird Barton Stone's understanding of God and also feature in Campbell's eschewing "abstract theological speculation" in favor of clear biblical language. Nevertheless, we also learn that Campbell could not abide discarding Christianity's Trinitarian moorings; he even maintained an unexpected (given his rationalist commitments) view of the Holy Spirit as a "personal existence," the "active, operating agent" in "all the works of God." By placing Campbell's commitments in concert with the Trinitarian assertions of the early church, Chapter Two builds a convincing case that the doctrine of the Trinity actually *safeguards* the devotion to biblical belief so valued by Churches of Christ, rather than enticing Scripture readers into needless abstraction and conjecture.

There are such gems to be found in all the chapters that follow. For instance, Chapter Three highlights the creation-affirming features of Campbell's and Lipscomb's eschatological positions, which are then set in relation to Eastern Orthodox understandings of salvation. The outcome is a biblically rooted view of evangelical discipleship as entailing "not only evangelism in the limited sense" (of convert-making) but more so a living into the human vocation of cocreating with God, which includes the eschatological drive toward "social transformation as well as the care, enjoyment, and protection of the creation."

Chapter Four is also intriguing in its appraising Church of Christ members' historic desires to be a "people of the Book," to pursue unity without downplaying Scripture's importance, and to embrace congregational interpretation. This chapter demonstrates how, when bankrupt strategies of legalist interpretation are replaced by theological approaches to understanding Scripture, those traditional Church of Christ commitments represent attractive alternatives to the pervasive "textlessness, apathy, and violent discourse" in contemporary Western culture. It is also worth noting that this transfigured hermeneutic emboldens "the local congregation's freedom to submit to the Bible over against institutional determinations" without driving toward anti-institutionalism—another siren song of the contemporary West. The liberty championed here is not a foolhardy freedom from each other, from the past, or from institutional arrangements; rather, it is a liberty afforded by learning to live with each other, a freedom "*not* to reject traditions that cohere with the text" (emphasis mine). Relatedly, the impetus is not toward a naive, anti-intellectualist insistence on the self-interpreting nature of the biblical text. Granted, the interpretive trajectory is, at heart, populist (it embraces the value of each congregant's engagement with Scripture). Nevertheless, by recognizing that the text does not self-interpret, it welcomes the help that careful scholarship *can* afford the community's interpretive efforts. In short, hierarches of responsibility are necessary within functional communities. But this vision of church governance is not one that supports top-down authoritarianism; rather, it endorses the servant-leader's charge to "equip" every member for "participation in God's mission."

On all accounts, Powell, Hicks, and McKinzie believe that the church is called to read the text and world through the "spectacles" of the Trinitarian God's story—a story codified in the creedal language of the Great Tradition and properly taken up in the mode of charitable conversation in community. They believe that when the interpretive process is undertaken in this fashion, Scripture "draws us into God's mission" through the power of the Spirit, thereby providing us with imaginations transformed for the sake of carrying out the work of God. Namely, this renovated imagination equips the church "to practice theological discernment for its ongoing participation in God's mission," where that participation is improvised in its polity, ethics, worship, and public communication, and where that discernment is always "concretely communal," integrating all members' diverse gifts for moving toward the redeemed community's missional *telos*.

Of course, this all sounds wonderful—and I hope that most of us can think of particular instances where we have seen something like this process actually born out. But, given how rare those instances are, one might also wonder how likely it is that we can consistently live out this vision of the local congregation: a community wherein all members submit to each other as they embrace Scripture as "provocateur" and "equipper," whereby they find the Holy Spirit transforming their collective vision through "critical self-reflection and ongoing recontextualization" while simultaneously illumining the "substantive essentials" needed for entering into mission in confidence and unity. If it is this straightforward, why do so many Christian communities experience internal discord so much of the time? Or, perhaps it is not so straightforward—perhaps the myth of biblical "perspicuity" still allures us when we muse over the metanarrative's power to draft us into God's drama and transform our imaginations.

We find ourselves in a difficult position. On the one hand, it seems that we must believe our collective dwelling with the Word can produce a sensibility that supports faithful improvisation in the unscripted situation. (We must believe it, that is, if we intend to go on giving credence to the corporate sanctification attested in 2 Corinthians 2:15 and to Scripture's role averred in 2 Timothy 3:16–17.) On the other hand, we would only be fooling ourselves if we do not remain uncomfortably aware of how messy our improvisational efforts tend to be. To come to terms with this, one only needs to try to offer an account of how eschatological expectation—defined here as the sensibility that "gives direction to and motivation for a life of discipleship in the present"—should speak into interecclesial conflicts concerning the church's stance on poverty, political partisanship, women in ministry, or same-sex marriage. In such instances, we quickly come face-to-face with the fact that "listen[ing] to each other without marginalizing some or ceding responsibility to a few" can be a supremely difficult task. And the proper way forward is not necessarily illumined by the lights of the "Great Tradition"—after all, the various liberation theologies have taught us nothing if not that sanctioned church teaching can be deaf to the voices of those on the social and political margins.

The situation is challenging, certainly. But we have nothing to gain from giving up on the promise of sanctification. And, provided that we are vigilantly realistic about our problems—that we, in fact, embrace such vigilance itself as a means of sanctification—we have everything to gain from placing our hope in the resurrecting power of the Spirit who enlivens us. In view of that hope, we could say that the gift of *Discipleship in Community* is its authors inviting us to move toward the ideal, delineating eschatological trajectories into which we may seek to step together. Thus framed, the resounding call to "unity in essentials, freedom in nonessentials, and charity in all things" spurs us to get serious about dwelling with the Word theologically, struggling together to identify the essentials and to cultivate the virtues of charity, rather than expecting a few catch-all books to provide tidy solutions for the complexities of discipleship in the present.

To that end, one of the most promising features of Powell, Hicks, and McKinzie's work lies in its emboldening readers to take up a "higher" view of material bodies—both individual/corporeal and communal/corporate—than present-day Stone-Campbellites inherited from their rationalist forebears. In these authors' view of things, our physical urges and intuitions are not inevitably at war with our minds, the source of a slippery slide into subjectivity; rather, as the person engages in missional actions and receives the sacraments, her whole self becomes a medium of cooperation with the Holy Spirit's promptings. Likewise, the communal body is not merely a site of potential groupthink to be scrutinized for idolatry; instead, it can be the discursive setting wherein theological confession is refined, and wherein attempts at worship are cultured by trial, thus bequeathing to us the hard-won gifts of teaching and practice cultivated over time.

If such bodily touchpoints really are resources for inviting divine direction, then they beg us to continually consider how we might open ourselves to the Spirit's influence through intentional, embodied practices—not only by plumbing the depths of Scripture together, but also by physically showing up in the ways outlined in Matthew 25:34–36. After all, as my teacher M. Douglas Meeks used to say, it is in feeding the hungry that we become aware of the systems that prevent people from being fed; it is in visiting the sick that we discover how the healing systems need reform; it is in visiting the prisons that we find out what life inside them is like and what is keeping people there. Sometimes we can only discover a way forward by going ahead and fumbling toward the eschaton.

As we seek to invite the Spirit in and through our bodily performances, we might also find that—in a world of textlessness, apathy, and violent discourse—the simple act of weekly gathering can also be occasion for being formed in the likeness of Christ. On this account, the early Stone-Campbell notion of the "Lord's day" or assembly of the church as sacrament is worth bringing to the fore. If a sacrament is a material reality that simultaneously represents the gospel and offers a graced means of participating in eschatological reality, the assembly is rife with sacramental potential: here, we find the bodies of believers, serving each other the symbolic flesh and blood of Christ at the Lord's Table, opening themselves to the mystery and grace of encountering each other and Christ himself as one unified body. In most Churches of Christ, we also hear those bodies joining voices in a cappella singing—not as a means of clinging to dusty legalism (though it *can* be that, for some) but in confidence that it is the Spirit of God who is in our midst, be we tone-deaf or operatic, making beautiful our praise-offering. As Karl Barth said of a cappella singing, "It might be argued that in this way the community's praise of God is embedded by anticipation in that of the whole cosmos, to which the cosmos is undoubtedly called and which we shall unquestionably hear in the consummation."[1] In such moments of bodily communion, we may give our whole selves over to dispossessed love of the Three-in-One who takes us as we are—who bears with us in our faithlessness; who empowers us for love of the stranger, of the enemy, of even our estranged selves; who transfigures our imperfect offerings into tokens of resurrected beauty.

Lauren Smelser White is an assistant professor of theology at Lipscomb University in Nashville, Tennessee.

---

[1] *Church Dogmatics* IV.3.2, trans. G. W. Bromiley (Edinburgh: T&T Clark, 1962), 867.

RESPONSE

Stanley Talbert

> *Christian theology is a theology of liberation. It is a rational study of the being of God in the world in light of the existential situation of an oppressed community, relating the forces of liberation to the essence of the gospel, which is Jesus Christ.*
>
> —James H. Cone, *A Black Theology of Liberation* (2010)

I began my academic theological journey at Union Theological Seminary the same year seventeen-year-old Trayvon Martin was fatally shot. Like continuous firecrackers against the dark canvas of a Fourth of July night, the idolatry of white supremacy concretized itself as bullets against black bodies. As I sat in my theology classes, the social climate pressed me to reflect on the meaning of the gospel for a world where people were easily disposable by the state. At that time, I wrestled with what it meant for the nation and even communities of faith to stand with God while also standing on top of the crushed and bleeding.

My deep engagement with liberation theologies (especially black liberation theology) and postcolonial biblical studies demonstrated that liberation is the essential message of the gospel of Christ. God's radical presence in the incarnation of Jesus of Nazareth is the embodiment of God's liberation for God's people. No North American theologian has emphasized God's liberation in Jesus Christ more than James H. Cone. For Cone, liberation is not an incidental characteristic of the gospel; it is God's central message of the gospel. Cone was right in exclaiming that Christian theology is a theology of liberation. As such, *any* theological vision in twenty-first-century America must center liberation in its vision. Discipleship then becomes the participation in the *liberation work* of God, as expressed in Scripture.

Discipleship in Community invites readers to contemplate the theological commitments of the Stone-Campbell movement and to "a life of simple, authentic discipleship," which is central to the Stone-Campbell movement. The historical emphases on biblical studies, ecclesiology, and ministry in the Stone-Campbell legacy highlight the importance of *Discipleship in Community*, with its attention to theological reflection and discourse. The authors claim that discipleship is the "orienting theological concern of the Stone-Campbell movement and Churches of Christ." In this way, the book initiates a return to what is fundamentally important in the Stone-Campbell tradition—discipleship.

At particular moments, *Discipleship* demonstrates the entanglement of discipleship and liberation by focusing on David Lipscomb's concern for the sick and the poor (even to the point of shaping his ecclesiological praxis), God's concern for those on the margins exemplified in the ministry of Jesus, and the ecclesiological participation in the liberation of the oppressed (Isaiah 61 and Luke 4). These moments are some of the essential parts of the book because they show that liberation is tied to discipleship. To be a disciple of Jesus Christ is to be concerned about the spiritual and physical liberation of God's people.

Regarding mission in the Stone-Campbell movement, the authors challenge Churches of Christ "to return to Scripture in order to recapture the missional theology of the first-century church," while also accounting for the colonial practices embedded in the missional work of Churches of Christ. The critique of the colonial practices of Churches of Christ regarding missions is a vital critique if discipleship is to be shaped by the liberation of the gospel. Theologian Willie Jennings's *The Christian Imagination* shows how warped visions of Christian missions misjudged, misplaced, and mistranslated many people.[1] The dislocation of people from their land, the tragedy of translation, and false intimacy are some ways in which the Christian imagination is warped. Jennings shows how Christians inverted the relationship between Christian discipleship and racial judgment. Whereas Christian discipleship should have shaped pedagogical practices, racial optics and judgment determined Christian discipleship and missional practices. Churches of Christ would do well to interrogate the ways that its focus on discipleship has been determined by racial optics.

Although these moments of discipleship and liberation occur throughout *Discipleship in Community*, the Stone-Campbell tradition would benefit significantly by making liberation the central focus of discipleship. In this way, participation in the triune life of God animates the community of believers to be witnesses of God's liberation in our world. Theologian Jacquelyn Grant argues for a model of discipleship that focuses on the empowerment of those who have been ostracized by society and even the church.[2] I agree with Grant, who claims discipleship should provide adequate

---

[1] Willie Jennings, *The Christian Imagination: Theology and the Origins of Race* (New Haven, CT: Yale University Press), 2010.
[2] Jacquelyn Grant, "The Sin of Servanthood," in *A Troubling in My Soul: Womanist Perspectives on Evil and Suffering*, ed. Emilie Townes (Maryknoll, NY: Orbis Press, 1993), 214.

substance for liberation and should animate believers to stand against oppression wherever it is found.

The life and legacy of Dietrich Bonhoeffer are a testament to a life of discipleship that is rooted in liberation. In *The Cost of Discipleship*, Bonhoeffer says,

> When the Bible speaks of following Jesus, it is proclaiming a discipleship which will liberate mankind from all man-made dogmas, from every burden and oppression, from every anxiety and torture which afflicts the conscience. If they follow Jesus, men escape from the hard yoke of their own laws, and submit to the kindly yoke of Jesus Christ.[3]

For Bonhoeffer, following Jesus is about liberation. Here, discipleship is not an easy accomplishment; it is costly. As a German theologian in the wake of Nazism, Bonhoeffer knew the cost of discipleship, losing his life while taking a stand against Hitler. Christian discipleship should empower followers to take a stand even when that stand involves risking it all.

Discipleship in Community attends to the problems of disorientation, identity crises, and transition in the Stone-Campbell tradition. Although these are legitimate concerns that need attention, the Stone-Campbell tradition must reckon with the catastrophes associated with white supremacy, violence, gender, and economic oppression. These catastrophes (among others) dramatize the need for a discipleship that not only returns to the core message of the Stone-Campbell movement but also pushes the movement toward the liberation movement of Jesus Christ.

The tragedies and protests surrounding the deaths of black and brown citizens in the United States revealed an identity crisis

---

[3] Dietrich Bonhoeffer, *The Cost of Discipleship*, 2nd ed. (London: SCM Press, 1959), 40.

among Churches of Christ. Although a few churches invested themselves into the work of liberative discipleship by participating and organizing against brutality and violence, many remained silent, and others created a false dichotomy between worship and protest. Some churches in the Stone-Campbell tradition were unable to imagine how discipleship is rooted in the work of liberation and justice.

When Botham Jean was killed in his home by an off-duty police officer, I knew it was a call to discipleship, particularly for Churches of Christ. Botham was a beloved brother, friend, son, and student who led worship at the Dallas West Church of Christ and attended Harding University. Many of Botham's friends, family, and professors attested to his kindness and his gift of ministry through singing. Botham led worship the Sunday before his life was taken. The violence against Botham was shared by a community who participated in worship with him. Because Botham was a member of the Stone-Campbell tradition, we must question how Botham's life and death shape our understanding of discipleship in this current moment. How will Churches of Christ and its institutions stand with Botham's family in the pursuit of justice? Although discipleship requires reconciliation, if the tradition focuses on liberation, reconciliation will take place.

Discipleship in Community ends with theological (creedal) commitments aimed to help disciples follow the path of Jesus. The commitments help followers remember how they participate in the mission of the triune God, in the community of believers. I hope that these commitments will animate a praxis of liberation where the creeds lead to transformative deeds.

Stanley Talbert is a Seaver Faculty Fellow at Pepperdine University in Malibu, California.

RESPONSE

Carson E. Reed

In this response, I seek to identify ways in which the proposals of *Discipleship in Community* matter for congregational ministry and mission. This is not a full book review, but rather a focused engagement regarding the practical and contextual realities that the book addresses. I see my task as taking the conversation that the authors have begun into the congregations asking questions about identity, sustainability, and mission in a rapidly changing cultural environment.

The authors seek to redefine and reclaim significant elements of the Stone-Campbell DNA to foster a vision for the future of Churches of Christ. In some ways, this book articulates a *ressourcement*—a move to deepen a tradition by going back to the source and looking at what has come to us in new and fresh ways.[1] I am sympathetic to this move; indeed, such work is a necessity to each

---

[1] *Ressourcement* was defined by the Catholic poet Charles Péguy as a movement "from a less perfect tradition to a deeper tradition, an overtaking of depth, an investigation into deeper sources, a return to the source in the literal sense." Nicholas Healy, "Evangelical *Ressourcement*," *First Things* 213 (May 2011): 56.

successive generation of church leaders. Churches of Christ are at a critical juncture with an ever-greater number of congregations in decline. So the question of the past's gifts to the present for the sake of the future is a pressing one.

This book represents well the work of reclamation—not for the sake of the past but for the sake of the future. And the authors identify useful and important threads that make up the tapestry of Churches of Christ. Using the lens of practical theology and the realities of congregational life and witness, I wish to identify two ways in which this book does its work of reclamation—the way of appropriating the past with a strong sense of *continuity* and the way of appropriating that the reflects a *discontinuity*. I will then offer some trajectories for practice in congregational life.

CONTINUITY

By *continuity*, I wish to affirm both the conclusions the authors are drawing from their historical work and theological reflection and the way in which it serves congregational life and practice. One such example is the chapter on sacramental theology. The theocentric focus on baptism and the Lord's Supper not only offers a robust theology; it also helps embody faith in participatory practices. Doing and believing—what we practice and what we believe—shape and form disciples and congregations.[2] Ministers and church leaders can often neglect the power of leveraging practices in a way that invites congregations to embrace faith and embody it.

Likewise, the book raises points of continuity with the Stone-Campbell legacy of the practice of ministry in the dynamics that intersect with the role of Scripture shaping the life and well-being of congregations. Focusing on the nature of Scripture, the book

---

[2] Miroslav Volf, "Theology for a Way of Life," in *Practicing Theology: Beliefs and Practices in Christian Life*, ed. Miroslav Volf and Dorothy C. Bass (Grand Rapids, MI: Eerdmans Publishing, 2002).

proposes six functions that Scripture exercises in shaping Christian identity. These functions are largely continuous with the heritage of Churches of Christ, though they might well be contested by some readers. Yet the authors poignantly identify the reality that narratives matter and the multiple narratives in play within any given congregation need to be rooted in the narrative of Scripture and the Christian tradition.

I think readers of this book can both affirm the continuity yet also feel tension with some parts of the DNA in the way one particular narrative plays itself out—namely, the narrative of how Scripture is simple and can be easily understood by all. Thus, the authors rightfully suggest the useful and time-honored practices of preaching, communal reading of Scripture, and thoughtful study of Scripture. Such practices possess transformative power and can facilitate discipleship and congregational vitality.[3]

DISCONTINUITY

By *discontinuity*, I seek to identify elements of the book's argument where the appropriation of the past seems stretched. In these areas, I am in significant agreement with the authors of the book as they seek to articulate a future direction for Churches of Christ. However, I am less confident about the coherence of the past DNA with the trajectories they propose. To point out such discontinuous spaces with regard to practical theology highlights the need for Churches of Christ to recognize that new strands of DNA may well be necessary for mission and ministry in the twenty-first century. Likewise, I raise these perceptions of discontinuity because congregations may inadvertently neglect the degree of theological

---

[3] Carson E. Reed, "The Bible Goes to Church: Performative Reading of Scripture and Communal Identity Formation," in *Reading for Faith and Learning: Essays in Honor of M. Patrick Graham*, ed. Douglas L. Gragg and John B. Weaver (Abilene, TX: Abilene Christian University Press: 2017).

imagination necessary for vibrant participation in God's mission in the world.

Indeed, the chapter on mission illustrates elements of discontinuity that may be present in the book. Certainly, the concept of missions (plural) was present in the thought world of Campbell, Stone, and others. However, living in a young, hopeful nation of the nineteenth century fostered a way of seeing evangelization and missions in very different ways than either early Christian practices or contemporary conversations about missional theology. Since Lesslie Newbigin's watershed work that prophetically called the Western church to recover a Trinitarian understanding of mission, significant new understandings are now in play.[4] Indeed, as the authors note, the priority of restoration thinking became the primary focus for early generations within Churches of Christ. A reductionistic understanding of restoration to perceived ancient practices led to sectarian postures that privileged a particularly white and American vision of Christian faith.

To recognize the distance between older expressions of mission work and a recovery of the mission of God invites contemporary congregations to examine commonly held assumptions and perhaps challenge elements of sectarian DNA present. This discontinuity, when recognized, also invites a humility in congregational leadership to reimagine congregational identity as grounded in the God who sends. To be clear, I am not critiquing the place where the authors lead with regard to mission, but congregations may mistakenly neglect the distance between the deep history of Churches of Christ regarding the relationship with the ideas of mission and restoration.

---

[4] Consider Lesslie Newbigin, *The Open Secret: An Introduction to the Theology of Mission* (London: Society for Promoting Christian Knowledge/Eerdmans, 1978), and *Trinitarian Doctrine for Today's Mission* (Edinburgh: Edinburgh House Press, 1963).

This discontinuity expresses itself in some related ways. The term *restoration* carries a lot of freight with a wide array of meanings. Within this book, the term *restoration* connotes the concept of the goal of conforming with Christ, of practices of the New Testament church, of the spirit of the early church, and perhaps of the ethos of the New Testament church. Yet such language creates some discontinuity with other understandings of restoration. I believe it makes a big difference to ask whether restoration is fundamentally a human endeavor or a divine one. To be fair, the authors do use restoration in ways that reflect God's action in renewal and reconciliation. But once again, the tension between two frames, or ways, of understanding restoration is problematic for missional renewal of congregational life.

This discontinuity continues to show itself in various ways. For example, as the authors helpfully note, Churches of Christ have often ignored the Holy Spirit. Guidance for congregational life and practices are largely governed by looking to the past—to particular interpretations or readings of Scripture—since the focus is on the restoration of New Testament practices and teachings. This emphasis on *restoring* continues to press against the practices of discernment and paying attention to the active, "in the present" presence of the Holy Spirit.

Likewise, the return to the ancient order can inadvertently push against the eschatological reality of the larger story of God. Churches of Christ have practiced a deep commitment to the exegetical work of knowing and interpreting Scripture and utilizing the past. So when a congregation faces a new challenge—a changing neighborhood, controversial ethical issues, the multicultural and global environment—the natural move is to explore the immediate and distant past. Yet the full gospel story, the eschatological vision the authors articulate so well, argues for an additional move. That move is to see the future—God's future—as an authoritative source for understanding our present context. So, the language of restoration (looking backward) can limit congregational faithfulness to the present (God's presence through the Holy Spirit) by sadly avoiding the resources of the full and vibrant story of God (that includes the ushering in of a new age).

But if *restoration* is grounded fully in the triune God's action, then the term leads congregations forward toward the eschatological reality of God's preferred future to live holy lives of the Spirit. Congregations will be less likely to fall into the legalistic or sectarian frames of thinking that emerge when restoration rests on human practices. Such a move does not neglect Scripture as the witness of the early church. Rather, when we recognize that early Christians, like contemporary Christians, are seeking to pursue God's renewal, we will hold both the past and the future with imagination and hopefulness.

Similarly, ministerial practice will find points of discontinuity in conversations about the Believers Church tradition. Local, autonomous congregational churches matter. In contexts where pluralism and the decline of Christian witness are present, a number of researchers are demonstrating the vibrant possibility of congregations that are deeply formed by the participation and life-giving ministry of members.[5] Although many of the ways in which local congregations invest in the elements of the Believers Church tradition will look and feel similar to the heritage in Churches of Christ, there are some important points that create dissonance. Matters of contextuality, framed by robust theological convictions regarding the active presence of a Triune God,

---

[5] Christopher James, *Planting Churches in Post-Christian Soil: Theology and Practice* (New York: Oxford University Press, 2017); see also Paul Sparks, Tim Soerens, and Dwight Friesen, *The New Parish: How Neighborhood Churches Are Transforming* Mission, *Discipleship and Community* (Downers Grove, IL: InterVarsity Press, 2014).

will require theological and pastoral imagination that will lead churches to make choices to look more and more like current realities and less like a rural America of the nineteenth century.

TRAJECTORIES

By *continuity*, I am suggesting that elements exist within our tradition that easily move forward to serve new and emerging expressions of Churches of Christ. By *discontinuity*, I am suggesting other historical theological ideas from the past will require revision or alteration in light of the witness of Scripture and contextuality. What trajectories, going forward, might guide congregations in their commitment to be faithful—both to the past and to God's preferred future?

I would think the following ideas are particularly important to congregational life and mission. First, as the authors suggest, churches need to attend to an orthodox understanding of the Trinity. Without a fuller understanding of the Spirit, the capacity to think about present life and experience or to engage meaningfully in pursuing God's preferred future will continue to languish. Second, a commitment to coherence matters. Believing and doing are different, though clearly connected. Much of what languishes in congregational life finds root in a lack of coherence. A congregational leader can say that love or unity matter, but what is practiced is a very different set of values. Third, mission matters. Without a deep conviction that the local congregation as the body of Christ serves as witness to the gospel for the sake of God's work in the world, churches will continue to decline and falter.

So, as the authors suggest, *discipleship* creates the catalytic lens by which Churches of Christ must think about both past and future. And discipleship, with the corresponding virtues of humility, trust, and obedience in the Lord of the past, present, and future, is not only a hallmark of a bygone era but the central feature of a congregation poised to partner with God today.

Carson E. Reed is an associate professor of practical theology and Frazier Chair for Church Enrichment at Abilene Christian University in Abilene, Texas.

Appendix One

RULES OF FAITH AND ECUMENICAL CREEDS OF THE EARLY CHURCH

BAPTISMAL CREED FROM *THE APOSTOLIC TRADITION* 21.12–18 (CA. 215)

When the person being baptized goes down in the water, he who baptizes him, putting his hand on him, shall say: "Do you believe in God, the Father Almighty?" And the person being baptized shall say: "I believe." Then holding his hand on his head, he shall baptize him once.

And then he shall say: "Do you believe in Christ Jesus, the Son of God, who was born of the Holy Spirit and the Virgin Mary, and was crucified under Pontius Pilate, and was dead and buried, and rose again the third day, alive from the dead, and ascended into heaven, and sat down at the right hand of the Father, and will come to judge the living and the dead?" And when the person says: "I believe," he is baptized again.

And again the deacon shall say: "Do you believe in the Holy Spirit, in the holy church, and in the resurrection of the body?" Then the person being baptized shall say: "I believe," and he is baptized a third time.[1]

---

[1] All creedal translations are from Jaroslav Pelikan and Valerie Hotchkiss, eds., *Creeds and Confessions of Faith in the Christian Tradition*, 3 vols. (New Haven: Yale University Press, 2003), 1:50, 56, 61, 163.

IRENAEUS'S RULE OF FAITH FROM *PROOF OF THE APOSTOLIC PREACHING* 6 (CA. 180-200)

And this is the order of our faith and the foundation of the building and support of our conduct: God the Father, uncreated, incomprehensible, invisible, one God, Creator of all. This is the first heading [article] of our faith.

But the second heading is the Word of God, God the Son, Jesus Christ our Lord, who was revealed to the prophets, after the manner of their prophecy and as much as had entered into the preordination of the Father. By the Son's hand all things have come into being. And at the end of the time, to gather all together and sum up things, he willed to become man among men, visible and palpable, so as to destroy death and show forth life and perfect reconciliation between God and man.

And the third heading is the Holy Spirit, by whom the prophets prophesied and the fathers learned divine things and the righteous were led in the way of righteousness, who in the end of the time in a new manner, is poured out upon men, in all the world renewing man for God.

TERTULLIAN'S RULE OF FAITH FROM *PRESCRIPTIONS AGAINST THE HERETICS* 13 (CA. 203-10)

It is the rule of faith, moreover, that we now profess what we henceforth defend; that rule by which it is believed that there is one God only and no other beside him, Creator of the world, who brought forth everything from nothing through his Word, which was sent out before everything; and that this Word, called his Son, appeared in various visions in the name of God to the patriarchs, was heard always in the prophets, and finally was brought down by the Spirit and power of God the Father into the Virgin Mary, made flesh in her womb and was born from her as Jesus Christ. Thereafter, he proclaimed a new law and a new promise of the kingdom of heaven, performed great deeds, was nailed to the cross, rose again on the third day, was taken up to heaven and sat at the right hand of the Father, and sent in his place the power of the Holy Spirit who guides believers, and he will come again in glory to summon saints into eternal life and to the enjoyment of celestial promises, and to condemn the impious to perpetual fire, both parties being raised from the dead and having their flesh restored. This rule is from Christ.

NICENE CREED (381)

We believe in one God the Father all-powerful, Maker of heaven and of earth, and of all things both seen and unseen.

And in one Lord Jesus Christ, the only-begotten Son of God, begotten from the Father before all ages, light from light, true God from true God, begotten not made, consubstantial [*homoousios*] with the Father, through whom all things came to be; for us humans and for our salvation he came down from heaven and became incarnate from the Holy Spirit and the Virgin Mary, became human and was crucified on our behalf under Pontius Pilate; he suffered and was buried and rose up on the third day in accordance with the Scriptures; and he went up into the heavens and is seated at the Father's right hand; he is coming again with glory to judge the living and the dead; his kingdom will have no end.

And in the Spirit, the holy, the lordly, and life-giving one, proceeding forth from the Father [and the Son], co-worshiped and co-glorified with Father and Son, the one who spoke through the prophets; in one, holy, catholic, and apostolic church. We confess one baptism for the forgiving of sins. We look forward to the resurrection of the dead and life in the age to come. Amen.

Appendix Two

ALEXANDER CAMPBELL'S "SUMMARY VIEW OF THE CHRISTIAN SYSTEM OF FACTS"

God alone is self-existent and eternal. Before earth and time were born he operated by his Word and his Spirit. God, the Word of God, and the Spirit of God, participants of one and the same nature, are the foundations of *Nature, Providence,* and *Redemption.* In *Nature* and *Providence,* it is God, the Word, and the Spirit. In *Grace,* it is the Father, the Son, and the Holy Spirit. All creations, providences, and remedial arrangements display to us the co-operation of three divine participants, of one self-existent, independent, incommunicable nature. These are fundamental conceptions of all the revelations and developments of the Divinity, and necessary to all rational and sanctifying views of religion.

In the *Law* and in the *Gospel* these sacred and mysterious relations and personal manifestations of God are presupposed and assumed as the basis of the whole procedure. "God created *all things* by Jesus Christ, and for him." "The Word was in the beginning with God," "before all things," and "by him all things consist." "God created man upright." Man sinned: all became mortal: our nature became susceptible of evil. It is in this respect fallen and depraved. "There is none righteous—no, not one." God the Father has chosen men in Christ to salvation "through the sanctification of the Spirit unto obedience, and sprinkling of the blood of Jesus;" and "promised," to such, "eternal life before the foundation of the world."

Therefore, in "the fulness of time"—"in *due* time, God sent forth his Son, made of a woman"—for "the Word became flesh, and dwelt among us; and we beheld his glory, the glory as of an only begotten of the Father, full of grace and truth." "He showed us the Father." He died as a sin-offering—was buried, rose again the third day—ascended to heaven—presented his offering in the true Holy Place—made expiation for our sins—"forever sat down on the right hand of the Supreme Majesty in the heavens"—sent down his Holy Spirit—inspired his Apostles, who "preached with the Holy Spirit sent down from heaven"—persuaded many Jews and Gentiles that he was made "the author of an eternal salvation to all who obeyed him." He commanded faith, repentance, and baptism to be preached in his name for remission of sins to every nation and people under heaven.

All who "believe in him are justified from all things," because this faith is living, active, operative, and perfected by "obeying from the heart that mould of doctrine delivered to us." Hence such persons repent of their sins, and obey the gospel. They receive the Spirit of God, and the promise of eternal life—walk in the Spirit, and are sanctified to God, and constituted heirs of God and joint heirs with Christ. They shall be raised from the dead incorruptible, immortal, and shall live forever with the Lord; while those "who know not God, and obey not the gospel of his Son, shall perish with an everlasting destruction from the presence of the Lord and from the glory of his power."[1]

---

[1] Alexander Campbell, *The Christian System*, 2nd ed. (Pittsburg, PA: Forrester & Campbell, 1839; repr. Nashville: Gospel Advocate, 1970), 54–55.

CENTERED IN GOD

The Trinity and Christian Spirituality

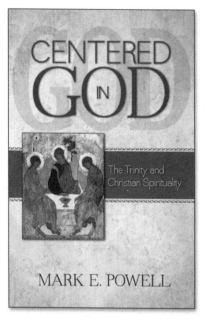

Mark E. Powell

In the early church, the Trinitarian vision of God was foundational for Christian identity, unity, and spirituality. For many Christians today, however, the Trinity is viewed as unreasonable and impractical. What exactly is the doctrine of Trinity and why is it so central to Christian faith and spirituality?

"We have an abundant supply of books on the Trinity that only professional theologians can understand. Mark Powell's *Centered in God* is quite different: a book on the Trinity that an ordinary Christian can easily understand and profit from. Scripturally rich, theologically accurate, and spiritually perceptive, this book is a tremendous resource not only for pastors, teachers, and students, but for all Christians who want to deepen their relationship with God."

—**Bruce D. Marshall,** Perkins School of Theology, Southern Methodist University

A GATHERED PEOPLE

Revisioning the Assembly as Transforming Encounter

John Mark Hicks, Johnny Melton, and Bobby Valentine

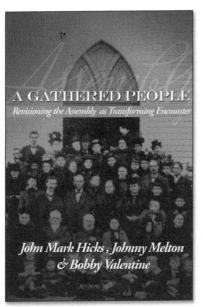

A Gathered People is an in-depth biblical, historical, and theological study of the Christian assembly or Lord's day. It examines Hebrew assemblies in the Old Testament, Christian assemblies in the New Testament, the changing nature of assemblies in Christian history, and the assembly in the Stone-Campbell heritage. As a companion volume to *Come to the Table* and *Down in the River to Pray*, this book completes a trilogy on the three "ordinances" of the Stone-Campbell Movement.

"Many think assembly is mostly something believers do for each other or seekers. Some conceive it primarily as a legal duty prescribed by God which we fulfill by performing the 'five acts of worship.' We argue that the Lord's Day assembly is fundamentally sacramental, that is, an encounter between God and his people for the sake of transformation and spiritual formation."

—From the Introduction

LEAFWOOD
PUBLISHERS
an imprint of Abilene Christian University Press